Second Edition

DEVELOPING LEADERSHIP ABILITIES

Arthur H. Bell, Ph.D.

Executive Director of MBA Programs

Dayle M. Smith, Ph.D.

Director of the Honors Program
School of Business and Management
University of San Francisco

Pearson

Boston   Columbus   Indianapolis   New York   San Francisco
Upper Saddle River   Amsterdam   Cape Town   Dubai   London
Madrid   Milan   Munich   Paris   Montreal   Toronto   Delhi   Mexico City
Sao Paulo   Sydney   Hong Kong   Seoul   Singapore   Taipei   Tokyo

Executive Editor: Sande Johnson
Editorial Assistant: Clara Ciminelli
Vice President, Director of Sales and Marketing:
  Quinn Perkson
Senior Marketing Manager: Amy Judd
Marketing Assistant: Robin Holtsberry
Project Manager: Holly Shufeldt

Art Director: Jayne Conte
Cover Designer: Bruce Kenselaar
Cover Photo: Getty Images, Inc.
Composition: GGS Book Services
Printer/Binder: Courier/Stoughton
Cover Printer: Courier/Stoughton

Every effort has been made to provide accurate and current Internet information in this book. However, the Internet and information posted on it are constantly changing, so it is inevitable that some of the Internet addresses listed in this textbook will change.

Library of Congress Cataloging-in-Publication Data

Bell, Arthur H. (Arthur Henry), 1946-
  Developing leadership abilities/Arthur H. Bell, Dayle M. Smith.
      p. cm. — (Neteffect series)
  Includes bibliographical references and index.
  ISBN-13: 978-0-13-715278-0
  ISBN-10: 0-13-715278-7
  1. Leadership.   2. Executive ability.   I. Smith, Dayle M.   II. Title.
  HD57.7.B448 2010
  658.4'092—dc22

                                        2009018906

www.pearsonhighered.com

10 9 8 7 6 5 4 3 2
ISBN 10: 0137152787
ISBN 13: 9780137152780

CONTENTS

PREFACE

In this thoroughly revised second edition, we have enriched your study of leadership by adding more topics on the cutting edge of best leadership practices:

- why servant leadership has replaced top-dog leadership in many organizations
- how to tell when leadership—including your own—is in danger of faltering
- how to delegate to those who are unwilling to take on new responsibilities
- how to adjust your leadership style to small groups and teams
- how to be a "leader of oneself" as a prerequisite for leading others
- tips on making leadership techniques flexible for changing circumstances
- how to transition between the roles of leader and follower
- how to use emotional intelligence as part of your leadership strategies
- why gender, culture, and other factors must be considered and understood by successful leaders
- how leadership responsibilities can be distributed throughout the organization
- how to use techniques to act swiftly to resolve conflict
- how social networking, YouTube, cell phones, and other technologies have influenced leadership options

And more. We have maintained our resolve to write a book you will want to read. Because you are no doubt busy (virtually every leader and leader-in-training is), we have highlighted the most crucial points in the book and included brief chapter summaries.

Perhaps most important, we have significantly increased the popular "Your Turn" opportunities throughout the book—space set aside for you to record your own reactions, experiences, insights, and questions. We envision a partnership between authors and readers in which we do our best to express current, important ideas about leadership and you do your best to respond personally and meaningfully to those ideas. Out of such a partnership, we believe, comes the real value of this short book: your opportunity for fast-track development as a leader.

We are gratified that the first edition of this book has been translated into many languages, and we extend sincere thanks to the many international business people, students, and professors along with our domestic readers who have advanced our thinking by their insightful letters and e-mails.

Acknowledgments

We thank the thousands of researchers and practitioners who have made the literature on leadership among the richest repository of thought in the field of organizational behavior and development. We especially acknowledge our many teachers at the University of Southern California and Harvard University.

Our colleagues at the University of San Francisco have supported this work with their encouragement, expertise, debate, stories, and friendship. A colleague's offhand remark in the hallway or question over coffee often proved catalytic in helping us see new aspects of our topic and better ways to communicate our ideas. Special appreciation goes to Dean Mike Duffy and Associate Dean Zhan Li at the Masagung Graduate School of Management, University of San Francisco, for their support of our work.

We would like to thank the following reviewers: Sally Gelardin, University of San Francisco, and George Nagel, Ferris State University.

Our thoughts on leadership have been deeply influenced by the experiences of actual leaders, including the many women leaders interviewed for Dayle Smith's book *Women at Work* (Prentice Hall, 2000). We thank corporate leaders at all levels at the following companies for allowing us to learn about their leadership successes and challenges: Charles Schwab, Citicorp, Sun Microsystems, Cost Plus World Market, American Stores, Artex Knitting Mills, Companion Health Insurance, the U.S. Coast Guard, Genentech, Kaiser Permanente, Johnson & Johnson, General Electric, Marriott Corporation, DuPont, Pacific Bell, Deutsche Telekom, British Telecommunications, China Resources, IBM, PaineWebber, Wells Fargo, the U.S. State Department, the Central Intelligence Agency, Colonial Williamsburg Foundation, California Federal Savings, the *Los Angeles Times*, Cisco Systems, Santa Fe, and Agilent Technologies.

We proudly dedicate this book with love to our first grandchild, Vincent Bell.

Art Bell
Dayle Smith
Belvedere, California

Other Books in this Series by Bell/Smith

Learning Team Skills

Motivating Yourself to Achievement

Interviewing for Success

Building Your Network through Communication

1

Surprising Facts About Leaders

GOALS

- understand that the skills and concepts discussed here are aimed at your leadership development
- recognize that leaders come in all shapes, sizes, and flavors
- learn how leadership as service to others provides a useful alternative to more ego-based forms of leadership

We want this short book to be more of a conversation than a lecture.

A quick glance through these pages will reveal more than 75 "Your Turn" invitations—spots in the book where we pause to listen (and ask you to listen as well) for your own response and feedback to leadership questions. Of course, we cannot hear what you have to say in a literal way. But by jotting down your thoughts—right in the book, if you wish or your instructor directs—you will help to create a conversation in which two sets of ideas are valued and recorded: both what we think about leadership and what *you* think about leadership. Together, these sets of ideas can help you select which leadership skills you want to make your own and learn how to go about developing them.

What we write in the following pages will mean little unless we've thought accurately and continually about you, the reader. Page by page, we have to ask ourselves whether we're holding up our end of the conversation by *giving you what you want* from a short book on leadership skills. We can't know, of course, your specific identity and circumstances—whether, for example, you're a student or someone already involved in a career, whether you're reading this book as part of an academic assignment or a company workshop, or simply for personal interest. But we can make three important assumptions about you. See if we're right:

1. You're quite busy. You don't want to listen to a long drone from Uncle Fred at the dinner table. You want us to get right to the point in plain language.
2. You're ambitious. You want to understand and use leadership skills to achieve your goals and perhaps help others achieve theirs.
3. You're practical. Although leadership theory probably interests you, you haven't picked up this book just to read about where the rubber meets the sky. You seek insight on how to develop and strengthen real-world leadership abilities that you can try out right away in your academic, professional, or social life.

If we're right about you, please read on. If not, you may want to look through the bibliography of other recent books on leadership to find one or more that fit your needs and interests. Or e-mail us at bell@usfca.edu with a description of your interests and the kind of book you seek. We'll do our best to help.

A SHORT BOOK ON A LARGE TOPIC

The Library of Congress catalog lists more than 8,000 books—including this one—written in the last 20 years on aspects of leadership. Stacked one on top of another, these books would form a tower (albeit a teetering one) higher than the Statue of Liberty.

So why one more leadership book, and a slim one at that? First, this book targets personal leadership development rather than the more common topic of leadership roles in business and other organizations. This book is about your own leadership development, not about corporate hierarchies or social structures. Second, this book contains several new perspectives on leadership that can't be found elsewhere in the towering stack. These new perspectives center on putting ego aside or, better said, delaying immediate ego needs for the sake of finding fulfillment in the accomplishments of one's followers. As grateful as we are to the extensive literature on leadership, we've also hatched several insights and techniques on leadership development in our many years of teaching and consulting. We're eager to share these new approaches with you.

But perhaps most important, this book is short enough that busy people—those likely to rise to leadership positions—will actually read it. We have tried to pack it full of valuable tips for leadership growth, ordered much like a menu from which you can choose those that appeal to your taste and style. We won't presume to tell you specifically what you should do to nurture your leadership potential. We can, however, present a banquet of leadership development choices and explain how each may be of use to you.

WHAT IS A LEADER?

This is not intended as a Zen question, such as "What is the sound of one hand clapping?" We're contemplating, as we invite you to, whether the question "What is a leader?" can be answered in any useful way. Of course, we could cheat a bit and reply, "A leader is one who leads"—but that simply begs the question.

YOUR TURN

Play along for a moment with a short experiment that may help us define a leader or perhaps show us why such attempts at definitions are difficult and risky. Please jot down the names of at least three friends or acquaintances you consider to be strong leaders. It doesn't matter for now whether they lead a huge company or a small club, whether they are related to you or are classmates or work associates. Simply choose individuals that for whatever reason come to mind when you are asked to list leaders you know.

1. _____

2. _____

3. _____

Now take a moment to think about what your three chosen leaders have in common. Do they have similar personalities? Are they especially sociable and well liked? Do they enjoy public attention and praise? Are they perpetually optimistic? Do they exude confidence? Do they have a commanding presence that, like a halo, makes them stand out as leaders?

We have conducted this "name-three-leaders" exercise in scores of companies and at several universities. When asked the questions in the previous paragraph, participants are usually somewhat surprised to find themselves answering, "Well, not really." Even a list of only three leaders usually muddies the water of defining the precise qualities of leadership. "The people I've chosen are all leaders," we find ourselves saying, "but they are very different personalities. They lead in different ways."

In this case, our failure to define the exact qualities of "the leader" is actually our first crucial success in understanding leadership:

INSIGHT 1

Leaders come in more varieties than crayons in the deluxe box. There simply is not a single set of qualities to be found in all leaders at all times.

Probably the most thorough investigation of this insight was undertaken by researchers Warren Bennis and Burt Nanus for their justly famous book, *Leaders: The Strategies for Taking Charge*. Over many months, Bennis and Nanus conducted in-depth interviews with nearly 100 corporate and public sector leaders. Perhaps these authors secretly hoped at the outset of these interviews to find the Rosetta Stone of leadership—the core traits that defined leaders or, put another way, lifted them above the herd of followers.

To their initial bemusement and eventual delight, Bennis and Nanus discovered that leaders did not fall uniformly into the mold of Superman or Wonder Woman. For every Charlton Heston figure leading an organization, there was also a Walter Mitty or a Vanna White. In sum, they write, "There was a great amount of diversity among the leaders. . . . Most were very ordinary in appearance, personality, and general behavior."[1] A similar conclusion was reached by Ralph Stodgill, a well-known leadership guru, after his painstaking review of scholarly works on the nature of leadership: "A person does not become a leader by virtue of the possession of some combination of traits."[2]

ROOM FOR US ALL

The insight that leaders don't share a common set of traits has great importance as a starting point for personal leadership development. Before we discuss that importance, we want to record what you think on this issue.

YOUR TURN

In the following space, please complete this sentence:

"The idea that leaders differ in personal traits makes me realize that . . .

_____

_____

_____

_____

_____

_____

The investigations of Bennis, Nanus, and Stodgill (and perhaps your own brief experiment in identifying three leaders) have virtually destroyed a centuries-old idea that "leaders are born, not made." Also known as the "peaks and valleys" theory of leadership, this notion would have us believe that out of the lowlands of human experience occasionally erupts a born-to-lead "peak" individual—a Joan of Arc, Winston Churchill, Franklin D. Roosevelt, Susan B. Anthony, Martin Luther King Jr., John F. Kennedy, and so forth. Biographers of these leaders often perpetuate the "peaks and valleys" mind-set by portraying their subjects as special from their earliest years—precocious in the cradle; head and shoulders above classmates in school; and marked for greatness by a gleam in the eye, a fire in the belly, and other forms of spiritual indigestion.

In most cases, this is hogwash. If it is our purpose not to praise Caesar but to bury him, we could compile for virtually any famous leader a compelling body of evidence showing the *ordinariness* of most of that leader's life experiences. Renowned leaders, it happens, often come from broken homes, have spotty or downright soiled academic records, make a mess of their personal lives, break trust with their friends, get caught in big and little lies, and otherwise walk a crooked path to their eventual distinction as leaders. The imported idea that these individuals were "born to greatness" is commonly a fabrication invented by those with a personal need or professional reason to worship.

INSIGHT 2

Leaders do not necessarily prove their leadership abilities at an early age or demonstrate leadership qualities in all areas of their lives.

LEADERSHIP AND DIVERSITY

As the 2008 presidential race made clear, leadership has no color, gender, or age restrictions. But making that point in a book is easier than applying it in life. Here's a case in point from a fast-food restaurant:

> The owner of Urban Burger had a tough decision to make. Two excellent employees, Linda (22) and Franklin (38), had both been with the restaurant for three years. They had both distinguished themselves as leaders among the other employees, consistently demonstrating superb customer service, careful attention to details, and a friendly attitude that made the workplace an enjoyable environment. When it came time to choose an assistant manager for the restaurant, almost all employees assumed that the owner would choose Frank. He was older than other employees and, in the same way that parents manage children, employees felt that Frank was the natural choice for management duties in the restaurant. Frank was also male, of course, and not a few employees figured that fact alone would cause the owner (also a male) to give the assistant manager position to Frank. These employees pictured a man as being more stern and less susceptible to "sob stories" from employees than a younger female manager, no matter how capable she had proven herself.
>
> Employees were stunned, therefore, when the owner announced that the new assistant manager was Linda. Frank accepted the decision graciously and congratulated Linda. She herself was surprised: "I didn't think I had much of a chance. Women usually don't win out in management competitions involving the other gender, and older workers just seem more 'management material' than younger ones. This promotion really encourages me and I'm going to work to deserve it."

Leaders not only arise from diverse backgrounds, but have to be careful not to fall back into old, prejudicial assumptions in the leadership decisions they made. Tom, for example, has to choose four team leaders for an important project at work. Will he consider only men from a majority ethnicity for the positions? Or will women and under-represented ethnicities have an equal chance, as judged by their talent?

One particular pitfall for leaders in this regard is the 10, 9, 8, 7 syndrome. It works like this: the leader considers himself or herself a 10, in terms of talent and the ability to guide and motivate others. But when it comes time for him or her to choose a "second in command" (a vice president, for example, in a company) he or she may make the mistake, even at a subconscious level, of choosing a person a bit less talented than he or she is, even if an equally talented or more talented person is available. Psychologists have explained this phenomenon as an unwillingness on the part of the "10" leader to create a competitive environment. The "10" leader wants someone who is smart, but not so smart that he or she contradicts the "10" leader and outshines him or her in front of others. Once the "9" employee is chosen, certain hiring duties fall to him or her—and the cycle repeats itself. Not wanting to be shown up by his or her own subordinate, the "9" employee hires an "8" in terms of talent and ability. The "8," in turn, hires a "7" and so forth down the slope, to the detriment of the company and ultimately to all those employed by the company.

Leaders must have the courage to select other leaders who are not "one step down" from themselves in talent and intelligence. Hiring one's equal may mean more frequent debates about particular decisions or courses of action. But so much the better for a progressive organization: important matters should be open for discussion and debate among intelligent people. Shutting down such discussion by playing the "Big Me, Little You" game in hiring does a disservice to all stakeholders in the organization. The boss and shareholders lose because the company does not perform as well as it could. The employees lose because they aren't encouraged to give frank feedback to those above them. Customers and the general public lose because the company (flawed by its core decision-making processes) can't produce an optimal product or service.

In short, not one of us is disqualified from leadership possibilities by our genes or life circumstances. In fact, often we can be surprised by finding strong leadership skills in someone we had written off as a "loser." Hermann Hesse makes this point in his novella *A Journey to the East.* A group of full-of-themselves individuals are making a cross-continent pilgrimage under the sponsorship of a holy order. The only "nobody" on this difficult journey is a servant, Leo, who cheerfully waits hand and foot on the pilgrims. Halfway through the journey, however, Leo mysteriously disappears. The pilgrims, all with enlarged egos, quickly fall into arguments over who should perform the menial work necessary to keep the pilgrimage on track. In the heat of anger, they soon abandon the journey altogether and each of the would-be pilgrims sets out alone into the wilderness, many to disaster.

Living hand to mouth, one pilgrim wanders for several years. In rags, this pilgrim fortunately crosses paths with the former servant Leo, who guides him to the care and protection of the holy order that had originally sponsored the pilgrimage. As he and Leo approach the gates of the order, the pilgrim is amazed to see Leo welcomed with honor and joy by all. Far from being a menial servant, Leo has all along been the revered leader of the order.

The concept of servant leadership, as conveyed by the Hesse story, runs counter to the powerful tradition of the egocentric leader—that is, the leader whose motives are intended in large part to punish those who oppose his or her will and reward those who obey him or her. In either case, the leader's ego is the supreme court that decides whether blame or praise is in order for others.

By contrast, the servant leader bases judgments on *what is best for the group in relation to attaining its goals.* At times, this suppression of personal ego and selfish motives may be quite obvious, as when a corporate leader voluntarily offers to take a miniscule salary while his or her company is recovering from difficult economic times. At other times, the actions of the servant leader may be hidden almost entirely, observed only by those who are approached by the servant leader and asked, "How can I help you do your job?"

Being a servant leader does not mean giving up ego-satisfying experiences. Rather, the servant leader derives fulfillment and personal satisfaction by seeing his or her supportive role pay dividends in the confidence, creativity, and productivity of others. (This same phenomenon can be observed in many parents, whose most lasting satisfaction comes from the influence they have had on the lives of their children, not on the trophies of one kind or another that they themselves have won in the course of their lives.)

YOUR TURN

What does this parable suggest about styles of leadership? In the following space, jot down your own conclusions.

"I think Hesse portrays Leo as a servant to make the point that . . .

_____

_____

_____

_____

_____

_____

LEADERSHIP AS SERVICE TO OTHERS

Although leaders don't necessarily do dishes and take out the trash, they nevertheless perform a valuable service for others. Like Leo, they do what is required to keep members of the group moving forward in relative harmony.

INSIGHT 3

Some leaders prefer to avoid the spotlight in order to support the group as a servant-leader.

Note how different this perspective of leadership is from the more common view of the leader as grand potentate—one to be served rather than one who serves. Hesse asks us to think about the kind of leader who is mission focused rather than ego focused. The Leo leader finds satisfaction not in the amount of attention he can command from others (the "worship" syndrome) but instead in the amount of help he can give to assist the group in achieving its goals. Like Leo, the best leader can sometimes be almost invisible.

Confucius had a similar insight in mind in his reflections on leadership:

"Of the hated leader, the people say 'He ordered us to work.'
Of the respected leader, the people say 'He encouraged us to work.'
Of the beloved leader, the people say 'We did it ourselves.'"

YOUR TURN

Think of a leader among your acquaintances who doesn't seek personal glory but instead seems to find satisfaction in simply helping the group do its best. Use the following space to record your thoughts about this leader.

"I consider _____ a servant-leader because . . .

_____

_____

_____

_____

_____

_____

LEADERSHIP PLURAL

The very word *leader* conjures up for most of us a singular image—one man or woman who stands at the head of a parade of followers. That need not be the case, as evidenced by the "leadership teams" at or near the top of most large corporations. A leadership team is composed of individuals who know that, by themselves, they lack the time, energy, and expertise to make consistently wise decisions on behalf of the company. By relying on other team members, these individuals gain from the counsel, perspective, and different skill sets of the rest of their fellow leaders. Although the leadership team does not act robotically with a single voice, it functions much like a president's cabinet in sharing insights and coming up with the best recommendations possible.

At Apple Computer, it has been common practice for decades to treat all the members of entire work teams as leaders. "If you were to step into the plant today," one Apple employee told us, "you probably couldn't pick out the bosses from the other workers. Especially when we're really engaged in an exciting project, we all feel like leaders within our individual areas of influence and expertise. It wouldn't work to have one top honcho in the group telling the rest of us exactly what to do. Most high-tech projects are too complex for any one individual to call all the shots. It takes a shared approach to leadership to bring out the best in each of us and make us feel that our thoughts and actions really matter to the success of the project. I'm not saying that on the organizational chart Apple doesn't have its company leaders. I'm just saying that most of us feel like leaders because we're treated that way."

WHERE DO LEADERS COME FROM?

So far we have painted a purposely indistinct picture of leaders and what makes them tick. No genetic or social background is a surefire breeding ground for leaders. No particular set of personality traits can account for leadership potential or predict which individual will become a leader. No one leadership style is ideal for every situation—for every praise-seeking leader there is, thankfully, also a praise-avoiding leader like Leo. Nor is leadership a constant feature of an individual. Today's leader can be tomorrow's follower, then rise again in the future to leadership status.

One of the most poignant depictions of such "out-of-nowhere" leaders appears in Piers Paul Read's novel *Alive* (perhaps more familiar from the movie of the same title). Read recounts the dilemma of 28 survivors of a jetliner crash high in the Andes. Marooned in deep snow with only a broken section of fuselage for protection, these individuals depend on group morale and unity for their very survival. Those with high-status leadership records from the past ironically have little to offer the group and are the first to perish from cold and hunger. Just as ironically, a shy, unassuming boy named Parrado becomes the steadying leader for the desperate group and perhaps the person most responsible for their eventual survival. No one would have predicted that Parrado would rise to heroism as the most trusted and loved leader among the survivors. In the years following their rescue, Parrado returned to a quite unremarkable life as one more willing to be led than to lead.[3]

TRANSITIONING FROM LEADER TO FOLLOWER AND BACK AGAIN

Ironically, good leaders often make the best followers. Leaders know the difficulties of guiding and supporting others—and therefore work well as followers in understanding intuitively the burdens shouldered by the leader and the resulting patience required by the followers.

There is no shame for a leader in taking his or her place as a follower (as, for example, when an academic dean decides to give up administrative work and return to the teaching faculty). Leadership is simply a skill set that can be "turned on" for a specific use, but just as easily set aside for another skill set, that of the follower. Obviously, we blur this picture at times by according status and accolades to leaders while ignoring their followers almost entirely. But this mistake is usually remedied when leaders get a chance to give credit where credit is due, whether at the Oscars, the Baseball Hall of Fame, or the Nobel Prize ceremony: leaders invariably thank their teams, without whom their achievements would have been impossible.

INSIGHT 4

Leaders often rise to the occasion and thereafter return to the role of follower. No one leads at all times and in all circumstances.

A MENU OF CHOICES FOR LEADERSHIP DEVELOPMENT

Are we saying that nothing can be known or predicted about leaders or leadership in advance—that leaders simply burst onto the scene like stellar supernovae, only to fade as quickly as they flared? If this were the case, a book on the *development* of leaders would be pointless indeed.

So let's be clear about our plan: although a single, lockstep path toward leadership abilities can't and shouldn't be recommended, we can set out a *menu of leadership skills* from which you can shape your own development as a leader. The areas of leadership skills you choose to emphasize in your development will be very much according to the leadership opportunities you seek and your own personality and style as a leader. That style, of course, can grow over time. To help you extend your range of leadership options, Chapter 2 provides a self-assessment instrument that estimates your leadership tendencies based on personality factors. The adage "Know thyself" applies no less to leaders than to philosophers.

With that self-knowledge in hand, you can use the leadership skill sets described in Chapters 3 through 10 to augment areas in which you already have significant leadership skills and to fill in those areas where your skills may be less developed:

- expressing leadership vision (Chapter 3)
- leadership by listening (Chapter 4)
- leadership by building relationships and teams (Chapter 5)
- leadership by defining problems and reaching solutions (Chapter 6)
- leadership by motivating (Chapter 7)
- leadership by delegating tasks and responsibilities (Chapter 8)
- leadership by managing conflict (Chapter 9)
- leadership by supporting and empowering participation (Chapter 10)

Each chapter, including this one, concludes with a "Summing Up" section to highlight key points.

Instrument for Reflection and Discussion

"QUALITIES I ADMIRE IN A LEADER"

Directions: *We each encounter leadership in various spheres of our experience, ranging from our place as members of the entire human community to our life as citizens of a particular country, state, city, neighborhood, school, social group, and family.*

In each of the following questions, circle the letter of the one answer that comes closest to your true opinion and feelings among the choices. There is no single right or wrong answer.

After taking this instrument, complete the "Drawing Conclusions" exercise as a basis for personal reflection on qualities you admire in a leader and for discussion with others.

Note: *In discussion with others, you may find it useful to withhold the name of the leader you have in mind for each of these questions. Individuals may differ strongly in their attitudes toward particular leaders; as a consequence, discussion may devolve into unproductive arguments about "who's right and who's wrong."*

1. Among world political leaders now in power, I admire one leader in particular for this primary attribute:
   - (a) compassion
   - (b) will power
   - (c) ability to inspire others
   - (d) ability to achieve goals
   - (e) ability to listen and understand
   - (f) high moral standards
   - (g) ability to fight for a cause
   - (h) personal sacrifices made for others
   - (i) ability to overcome obstacles
   - (j) humility
   - (k) commitment to justice
   - (l) courage
   - (m) patience
   - (n) friendliness
   - (o) financial expertise and success
   - (p) intellectual brilliance
   - (q) other _____

2. Among world leaders now in nonpolitical roles, I admire one leader in particular for this primary attribute:
   - (a) compassion
   - (b) will power
   - (c) ability to inspire others
   - (d) ability to achieve goals
   - (e) ability to listen and understand
   - (f) high moral standards
   - (g) ability to fight for a cause
   - (h) personal sacrifices made for others
   - (i) ability to overcome obstacles
   - (j) humility
   - (k) commitment to justice
   - (l) courage
   - (m) patience
   - (n) friendliness
   - (o) financial expertise and success
   - (p) intellectual brilliance
   - (q) other _____

3. Among national political leaders now in power, I admire one leader in particular for this primary attribute:
   - (a) compassion
   - (b) will power
   - (c) ability to inspire others
   - (d) ability to achieve goals
   - (e) ability to listen and understand
   - (f) high moral standards
   - (g) ability to fight for a cause
   - (h) personal sacrifices made for others
   - (i) ability to overcome obstacles
   - (j) humility
   - (k) commitment to justice
   - (l) courage
   - (m) patience
   - (n) friendliness
   - (o) financial expertise and success
   - (p) intellectual brilliance
   - (q) other _____

4. Among national leaders now in nonpolitical roles, I admire one leader in particular for this primary attribute:
   - (a) compassion
   - (b) will power
   - (c) ability to inspire others
   - (d) ability to achieve goals
   - (e) ability to listen and understand

(f)   high moral standards
(g)   ability to fight for a cause
(h)   personal sacrifices made for others
(i)   ability to overcome obstacles
(j)   humility
(k)   commitment to justice
(l)   courage
(m) patience
(n)   friendliness
(o)   financial expertise and success
(p)   intellectual brilliance
(q)   other _____

5. Among state or regional political leaders, I admire one leader in particular for this primary attribute:
(a)   compassion
(b)   will power
(c)   ability to inspire others
(d)   ability to achieve goals
(e)   ability to listen and understand
(f)   high moral standards
(g)   ability to fight for a cause
(h)   personal sacrifices made for others
(i)   ability to overcome obstacles
(j)   humility
(k)   commitment to justice
(l)   courage
(m) patience
(n)   friendliness
(o)   financial expertise and success
(p)   intellectual brilliance
(q)   other _____

6. Among state or regional leaders now in nonpolitical roles, I admire one leader in particular for this primary attribute:
(a)   compassion
(b)   will power
(c)   ability to inspire others
(d)   ability to achieve goals
(e)   ability to listen and understand
(f)   high moral standards
(g)   ability to fight for a cause
(h)   personal sacrifices made for others
(i)   ability to overcome obstacles
(j)   humility
(k)   commitment to justice
(l)   courage
(m) patience
(n)   friendliness
(o)   financial expertise and success
(p)   intellectual brilliance
(q)   other _____

7. Among city or civic leaders where I live, I adinire one leader in particular for this primary attribute:
(a)   compassion
(b)   will power
(c)   ability to inspire others
(d)   ability to achieve goals
(e)   ability to listen and understand
(f)   high moral standards
(g)   ability to fight for a cause
(h)   personal sacrifices made for others
(i)   ability to overcome obstacles
(j)   humility
(k)   commitment to justice
(l)   courage
(m) patience
(n)   friendliness
(o)   financial expertise and success
(p)   intellectual brilliance
(q)   other _____

8. Among nonpolitical leaders in the area where I live, I admire one leader in particular for this primary attribute.
(a)   compassion
(b)   will power
(c)   ability to inspire others
(d)   ability to achieve goals
(e)   ability to listen and understand
(f)   high moral standards
(g)   ability to fight for a cause
(h)   personal sacrifices made for others
(i)   ability to overcome obstacles
(j)   humility
(k)   commitment to justice
(l)   courage
(m) patience
(n)   friendliness
(o)   financial expertise and success
(p)   intellectual brilliance
(r)   other _____

9. Among school or company leaders with whom I now have contact, I admire one leader in particular for this primary attribute:
(a)   compassion
(b)   will power
(c)   ability to inspire others
(d)   ability to achieve goals
(e)   ability to listen and understand
(f)   high moral standards
(g)   ability to fight for a cause
(h)   personal sacrifices made for others
(i)   ability to overcome obstacles

(j) humility

(k) commitment to justice

(l) courage

(m) patience

(n) friendliness

(o) financial expertise and success

(p) intellectual brilliance

(q) other _____

10. Among extended family members (including grandparents, parents, uncles, aunts, cousins, etc. I admire one person in particular for this primary leadership attribute:

(a) compassion

(b) will power

(c) ability to inspire others

(d) ability to achieve goals

(e) ability to listen and understand

(f) high moral standards

(g) ability to fight for a cause

(h) personal sacrifices made for others

(i) ability to overcome obstacles

(j) humility

(k) commitment to justice

(l) courage

(m) patience

(n) friendliness

(o) financial expertise and success

(p) intellectual brilliance

(q) other _____

DRAWING CONCLUSIONS

Please fill out each of these statements:

On the big stage of international and national leadership, I tend to value individual leaders for their qualities of (list) _____.

On the closer, more personal level of city, company, school, and family leadership, I tend to value individual leader for their qualities of (list) _____ _____.

If you observe a marked difference between these two sets of answers, please explain why you believe the difference exists: _____ _____.

If you do not observe a marked difference between these two sets of answers, please explain why you believe the same leadership qualities apply on the "big stage" as on the smaller stages closer to home: _____ _____.

Summing Up

Nothing prevents you from seeking to fulfill your potential as a leader. You are not out of the running based on genes, social status, personality traits, or any other circumstances. Learning new leadership skill sets will allow you to explore your leadership opportunities both on a small scale (perhaps within a student or work team) and on a larger scale (perhaps as one of the leaders of a student organization, work unit, or other group). The kind of leader you become depends on the kind of leader you want to become. Your leadership style will no doubt differ somewhat from the styles used by other leaders you know. By knowing the set of leadership skill options available to you, you can prepare yourself to lead effectively in changing circumstances.

2

Assessing Your Leadership Tendencies and Personality Factors

GOALS

- understand major personality differences among individuals
- determine one's own personality profile
- use personality information to build strong work teams, adjust to interpersonal differences, and choose activities that make the most of one's personality strengths

We each approach leadership challenges somewhat differently based on our differing personalities and life experiences. Understanding how your leadership approach may differ from someone else's is an immensely valuable first step in your leadership development.

THE ASSESSMENT

The following 60-question assessment takes about 15 minutes to complete. It will reveal dominant tendencies—in effect, what a person does most naturally—in eight common areas related to leadership style and personality type.

How can such information be useful to you? First, you can begin to predict how you will tend to approach challenges as a leader and where you are likely to experience interpersonal conflict with team members and others. If you discover, for example, that your leadership style relies on a high degree of *planning*, you probably will have difficulty (at first) dealing with someone content to *juggle* their way day by day. If your natural tendency is to lead by *thinking* about problems and solutions, you may experience stress in relating to team members who are just as devoted to *empathizing* or feeling their way into issues and situations.

Once you recognize ways in which your leadership personality differs from others, you can prepare to deal with those differences constructively. You can often avoid or lessen conflict with a team member by adapting your leadership approach to the personality needs of that person. A Juggler-employee, for example, going in to meet with a Planner-boss would be well advised to organize the presentation, create schedules and charts, and have all relevant details at hand.

As a leader, you can also use this instrument to help you build strong, flexible work teams. When a team is composed of members with complementary talents and tendencies, it is able to do more and respond to change more successfully. A team made up entirely of Planners, for example, would be highly organized but incapable of flexibility and crisis management. A team made up entirely of Thinkers might come up with intellectually complex arguments that don't appeal at all to most other human beings.

In both cases, the goal for an effective leader is to mix various personality tendencies among team members to build a strong, adaptable team.

Here's a brief description of each of the leadership and personality tendencies revealed in this assessment. No doubt you'll call to mind a person who matches each of these descriptions—and perhaps you will recognize yourself as well.

After reading about these eight types, take the short test and then score it to reveal your own dominant traits of personality.

The Member
- ❏ enjoys the company of others
- ❏ joins groups willingly
- ❏ avoids tasks that must be accomplished alone
- ❏ relies on consensus of the group for decision making
- ❏ values belonging, popularity, and the respect of others

The Self
- ❏ usually works alone
- ❏ joins groups reluctantly
- ❏ is suspicious about widely held beliefs and opinions
- ❏ seeks to measure up to personal standards rather than group norms

The Juggler
- ❏ is adept at minute-to-minute adjustments to changing conditions
- ❏ keeps many tasks in progress at once, all in a partial state of completion
- ❏ finds emergencies and unexpected developments energizing and challenging

❏ takes pride in the ability to "handle things" and "cope"

❏ perceives self as a rescuer for others who can't make quick decisions

The Planner

❏ likes to make patterns, schedules, charts, and organizational plans

❏ clings to plans even in the face of changing conditions

❏ resists information that contradicts existing plans

❏ perceives self as a bulwark against chaos

The Thinker

❏ seeks logical links between ideas, concepts, and facts

❏ postpones action until underlying causes are ascertained

❏ discounts the importance of intuition, emotional response, and irrational speculation

❏ values intellectual outcomes over practical outcomes

The Empathizer

❏ focuses on the emotional content of situations

❏ evaluates ideas and events according to how others feel about them

❏ perceives self as a caring, sensitive individual

❏ values gratitude, friendship, loyalty, and the respect of others

The Closer

❏ finds it easy to draw conclusions and make judgments and decisions

❏ feels impatient over delays for additional information or discussion

❏ ignores input that tends to postpone decision making

❏ perceives self as action oriented and powerful

The Researcher

❏ postpones decisions and actions to seek additional information

❏ craves certainty and is suspect of conclusions reached without full evidence

❏ ignores time and resource constraints to seek available knowledge

❏ finds it difficult to summarize or draw conclusions from complex information

❏ perceives self as a truth seeker in a world of intellectual compromisers

Assessment of Leadership and Personality Tendencies

Directions: Mark the score sheet at the end of this chapter (it's easiest to tear the score sheet out) with "a" or "b" for each question. If neither choice suits you entirely, choose the answer that comes closest to your answer.

1. At a social gathering connected with your work, do you usually
   (a) make conversation with many people?
   (b) make conversation with only a few people?

2. In learning about a new subject, do you prefer
   (a) to follow a step-by-step approach?
   (b) to grasp the big picture first?

3. Do your friends value you most for
   (a) what you think?
   (b) what you feel?

4. Have most of your important achievements been due to
   (a) a lot of hard work and a little luck?
   (b) a lot of luck together with hard work?

5. During your school years, did you consider yourself
   (a) popular with many people?
   (b) popular with a few people?

6. In learning about a company, would you prefer to know about
   (a) what employees are doing?
   (b) what employees may be able to do?

7. In meeting new people, do you form impressions based on
   (a) their appearance and actions?
   (b) personal chemistry?

8. When shopping, do you select items
   (a) impulsively?
   (b) carefully?

9. At work, do you prefer jobs that
   (a) bring you in contact with many people?
   (b) bring you in contact with only a few people?

10. In your opinion, is speculation about UFOs (unidentified flying objects)
    (a) interesting?
    (b) foolish?

11. Picturing yourself as a manager of others, would it be most important for you to be
    (a) firm?
    (b) friendly?

12. In arranging a deal between parties, would you
    (a) allow less important details to be left to good faith between the parties?
    (b) make sure all details were spelled out in writing?

13. Do you consider yourself to have
    (a) many close friends?
    (b) a few close friends?

14. Do you think national leaders should be
    (a) imaginative?
    (b) informative?

15. When someone confides in you about a personal problem, do you first
    (a) try to think of a solution?
    (b) feel sympathy?

16. In romantic relationships, should bonds and understandings between parties be
    (a) stated clearly?
    (b) left partially unstated?

17. When meeting strangers, do you
    (a) take the initiative in showing friendliness?
    (b) wait for signs of friendliness on their part?

18. Should children be raised to
    (a) enjoy childhood fantasies as long as possible?
    (b) learn practical skills and behaviors as soon as they are ready?

19. In general human affairs, is it most dangerous to show
    (a) too much emotion?
    (b) too little emotion?

20. In taking a test, would you prefer to deal with
    (a) questions with definite answers?
    (b) questions that are open-ended?

21. Do you find unexpected encounters with previous acquaintances
    (a) enjoyable?
    (b) somewhat uncomfortable?

22. Do you prefer a poem that
    (a) has many possible meanings?
    (b) has a single clear meaning?

23. In voting for a congressional representative, do you favor
    (a) an intelligent, cool-headed candidate?
    (b) a passionate and well-intentioned candidate?

24. Do you prefer dates that are
    (a) carefully planned in advance?
    (b) spontaneous?

25. In going out to lunch with friends, would you prefer to eat with
    (a) many friends?
    (b) one or two friends?

26. Do you feel that presidents of companies should be thoroughly
    (a) practical?
    (b) aware?

27. Would you prefer that acquaintances passing through your city
    (a) make specific arrangements to see you in advance of their trip?
    (b) call on the spur of the moment when they arrive?

28. When given a time for arrival at a social gathering, are you
    (a) usually right on time?
    (b) usually somewhat late?

29. When on the phone, do you usually
    (a) make most of the conversation?
    (b) respond in brief comments to what the other person is saying?

30. In general, would you prefer to read
    (a) a letter to the editor in a newspaper?
    (b) a modern poem?

31. Do you prefer to see movies that
    (a) reveal social conditions?
    (b) produce tears or laughter?

32. In preparing for a job interview, do you think you should prepare to talk more about
    (a) your achievements?
    (b) your future plans and goals?

33. If forced to accept dormitory accommodations during a conference, would you prefer to stay in a room
    (a) with a few other compatible conference participants?
    (b) alone?

34. In general, do you act on the basis of
    (a) the situation at hand?
    (b) your mood?

35. If you were hiring employees to work for you, should they be primarily
    (a) intelligent and creative?
    (b) loyal and dedicated?

36. In choosing a name for a child, should the parents
    (a) decide upon possible names well before the child is born?
    (b) wait until the child is born to settle upon the right name?

37. In making a consumer complaint, would you prefer to
    (a) call the company?
    (b) write the company?

38. When performing an ordinary work task, do you prefer to
    (a) try your own way of doing it?
    (b) do it in a traditional way?

39. In court, should judges
    (a) follow the letter of the law?
    (b) show leniency when they think it is appropriate?

40. If you are given a project to complete, would you prefer to turn it in
    (a) by a set deadline?
    (b) when you feel it is ready to turn in?

41. When introducing two of your friends who do not know each other, do you
    (a) tell them each a bit of information about the other?
    (b) let them make their own conversation?

42. Is it worse for an adult
    (a) to be too much in a routine?
    (b) to be too idealistic?

43. When you listen to speeches, do you prefer speakers
    (a) who prove their points?
    (b) who feel deeply about what they're saying?

44. At the end of the day, do you spend more time thinking about
    (a) what you did during the day?
    (b) what you will do tomorrow?

45. In planning your ideal vacation, would you choose a place where
    (a) you can meet family and friends?
    (b) you can be alone or with only one or two friends?

46. Which mental activity appeals to you more?
    (a) analysis
    (b) prediction

47. If you were president of a company, would it be more important to you that
    (a) all employees understood their job responsibilities thoroughly?
    (b) all employees felt part of the company family?

48. If you were a member of a project team, would you prefer to be most active during the
    (a) completion stage of a project?
    (b) initial conceptualization stage of the project?

49. In learning a new skill, would you prefer to be taught
    (a) as part of a small class?
    (b) one-on-one by a tutor?

50. In choosing leisure reading, would you be more likely to choose
    (a) a science fiction novel?
    (b) a historical novel?

51. In planning your career, should you
  (a) plan all career moves well in advance?
  (b) go with the flow of opportunity?

52. In writing an epitaph for an admired industry leader, should the inscription pay tribute to the person's
  (a) accomplishments?
  (b) aspirations?

53. Do you think the primary purpose of meetings in business is
  (a) to get to know one another and build team spirit?
  (b) to get work done as efficiently as possible?

54. Do you consider yourself as having a good head for
  (a) speculation?
  (b) facts?

55. Do you feel that the most important quality that employees can have is
  (a) individual initiative?
  (b) team spirit?

56. As a rule, do you consider yourself
  (a) a hard worker?
  (b) easygoing?

57. If your employer wanted to honor you at a luncheon, would you prefer that the luncheon be attended
  (a) by many company employees?
  (b) by your employer and only one or two others?

58. In general, do you think that quality that has been more valuable to human progress is
  (a) inspired insight?
  (b) common sense?

59. Do you think that the best thing that can be said about retiring employees is that
  (a) they were excellent at their jobs?
  (b) they cared about their fellow workers?

60. At the time they become engaged to be married, should a couple
  (a) set a definite date for the wedding?
  (b) leave the wedding date open for a while?

YOUR SCORE

On the score sheet at the end of this chapter, add up the columns to determine your relative tendencies in the eight leadership and personality categories. The higher your total within a particular column, the more intense is that trait in your leadership style and personality tendency.

By understanding your own personality traits, you can determine where you may fit in best as a team leader or team member. You can also locate areas of experience where you may tend to be "deaf" to the feelings or opinions of others. Finally, by understanding your own leadership and personality traits, you can predict with considerable accuracy the kind of people you may find difficult or hard to understand. A Self, who enjoys working alone, for example, may find it hard at first to accept the motives and habits of a Member, who insists on joining groups. To know one's traits is to prepare oneself to accept differences between people, then to create strategies as a leader to overcome the influence of those differences.

Remember that there is no "correct" or "best" profile for the workplace. All leadership and personality types have their place and usefulness. To interpret your scores most meaningfully, pick out your highest scores. These are the dominant traits in your personality as measured by this instrument.

A helpful exercise is to have a colleague or friend also take this instrument, then discuss differences in your scores and the different personality traits they represent. You may find yourself saying to the other person, "So *that's* why you act the way you do!" And the other person may well say the same thing about you. This sharing of personality knowledge can be the beginning of a new way of relating based on an appreciation of deep personality differences.

Summing Up

Each of us has personality tendencies that distinguish us from others in our school organizations and work lives. Using a personality assessment such as the one in this chapter, we can "place" ourselves on the following continua:

- Member vs. Self
- Juggler vs. Planner
- Thinker vs. Empathizer
- Closer vs. Researcher

Knowing our own personality tendencies and those of others gives us an opportunity to build complimentary work teams, plan for one another's differing needs, and choose activities most suited to our individual strengths.

Score Sheet

Directions: *After having circled your "a" or "b" answers for each item on the test, transfer your answers as checkmarks to this score sheet. Add the number of checks in each column to determine your personality tendencies. The higher the number of marks in a column, the more dominant that trait is in your personality.*

M = Member   J = Juggler   T = Thinker   C = Closer
S = Self   P = Planner   E = Empathizer   R = Researcher

M	**S**		**J**	**P**		**T**	**E**		**C**	**R**
1 a ❑	b ❑		2 a ❑	b ❑		3 a ❑	b ❑		4 a ❑	b ❑
5 a ❑	b ❑		6 a ❑	b ❑		7 a ❑	b ❑		8 a ❑	b ❑
9 a ❑	b ❑		10 a ❑	b ❑		11 a ❑	b ❑		12 a ❑	b ❑
13 a ❑	b ❑		14 a ❑	b ❑		15 a ❑	b ❑		16 a ❑	b ❑
17 a ❑	b ❑		18 a ❑	b ❑		19 a ❑	b ❑		20 a ❑	b ❑
21 a ❑	b ❑		22 a ❑	b ❑		23 a ❑	b ❑		24 a ❑	b ❑
25 a ❑	b ❑		26 a ❑	b ❑		27 a ❑	b ❑		28 a ❑	b ❑
29 a ❑	b ❑		30 a ❑	b ❑		31 a ❑	b ❑		32 a ❑	b ❑
33 a ❑	b ❑		34 a ❑	b ❑		35 a ❑	b ❑		36 a ❑	b ❑
37 a ❑	b ❑		38 a ❑	b ❑		39 a ❑	b ❑		40 a ❑	b ❑
41 a ❑	b ❑		42 a ❑	b ❑		43 a ❑	b ❑		44 a ❑	b ❑
45 a ❑	b ❑		46 a ❑	b ❑		47 a ❑	b ❑		48 a ❑	b ❑
49 a ❑	b ❑		50 a ❑	b ❑		51 a ❑	b ❑		52 a ❑	b ❑
53 a ❑	b ❑		54 a ❑	b ❑		55 a ❑	b ❑		56 a ❑	b ❑
57 a ❑	b ❑		58 a ❑	b ❑		59 a ❑	b ❑		60 a ❑	b ❑

Totals ❑ ❑   ❑ ❑   ❑ ❑   ❑ ❑

3

Expressing Leadership Vision

GOALS

- understand the nature of leadership vision
- generate ideas useful for leadership vision
- include meaningful action as part of leadership vision

Vision? For some people, the word may sound hopelessly otherworldly: St. Paul on the road to Damascus, Charlemagne and the burning cross in the sky, Joan of Arc and a transcendent glimpse of the destiny of France. However, we can turn down the volume on history and the movies to see vision in the common light of day. It's something we each experience in our daily lives as well as a skill that can be learned as part of our individual leadership development.

In this discussion of leadership, we don't have anything grandiose or particularly rare in mind. Vision for leaders in day-to-day life can be defined in simple, direct terms.

> **INSIGHT 5**
> Vision is a general idea of where you want to go and how you plan to get there.

Sometimes others follow your lead, as in the case of student government or management responsibilities at work. At other times, you find yourself on a more solitary journey, following your own vision and arriving at your goal alone.

In this sense, a leader's vision is quite literally like looking down the road to one's destination. Even if that destination cannot be seen clearly from the outset, a leader nevertheless has an idea of which road to take in order to reach the eventual goal or destination. But we don't want to make the mistake of branding leaders as prophets with mystical insights for which road to take. Leaders work at finding the correct path or direction.

YOUR TURN

Take a moment to jot down a vision you have had for creating something new or improving something that already exists. (For example, did you ever have an idea for improving an organization to which you belong?)

_____

_____

_____

_____

_____

_____

WHERE DOES VISION COME FROM?

Think for a moment about visionary leaders from U.S. and world history. How did General Patton decide during World War II which battles to fight and how many troops to commit? How did NASA settle upon a plan to put a person on the moon? How did Gandhi determine that his hunger strike and passive resistance would change the course of his nation's history? How did Volkswagen executives decide to build and market a retro version of the original VW Bug? With the advantage of hindsight, these leadership visions seem just the right thing at just the right time.

But at the decision-making moment, the leaders involved in these decisions did not know with absolute certainty that their visions—where they wanted to go and how they would get there—were correct or infallible. Privately, they probably agonized over the "what if's"—what if the troops were outmaneuvered, what if the rocket misfired, what if the hunger strike aroused no public interest, what if the new version of the Bug was ridiculed? For any thinking person, these kinds of thoughts accompany vision and lead to an important concept:

INSIGHT 6

Having vision as a leader does not mean closing one's mind to doubts and uncertainties.

A person who blindly pursues one idea with no regard for competing or conflicting ideas or circumstances is often labeled a fanatic or a fool rather than a leader. Effective leaders welcome information that may influence the direction or validity of their vision.

Let's take a practical example from student life. Richard T. is a student leader at Michigan State University. His particular vision for the improvement of student experience at that university involves a "safety net" system of counseling and other resources. He pictures a telephone, e-mail, and text message hotline that any Michigan State student can use day or night to reach immediate help with any kind of significant problem, whether emotional, financial, academic, or social. Counselors would field the calls and then route them to campus resource people best equipped to help the students involved. Richard envisions a student service with the motto, "There's no problem we can't solve together."

Sound like a good idea? Richard certainly thought so—until he circulated a letter to various student agencies describing his vision. To his surprise, some of the most important student service organizations on campus objected to his concept. The Suicide Prevention Hotline, for example, wrote this reply to Richard: "We oppose your plan because it delays immediate evaluation of students facing emotional crises. These students are usually not willing or able to explain their dilemma to one student operator, who then routes them to another student service for additional explanations. We feel it is of vital importance that emotionally distressed students contact us directly instead of through a unified service of the type you suggest."

At this point, Richard faces a choice that all leaders confront: do I abandon my vision at the first sign of objection, or do I "stick to my guns"? Neither of those alternatives is consistently useful for a leader. If Richard abandons his idea altogether, the good ideas within his vision are swept out with the not-so-workable ideas. On the other hand, if he sticks stubbornly to his original concept, he will undoubtedly face powerful political enemies on campus that may well be able to squelch his vision entirely.

YOUR TURN

Look back to the vision you described in the first "Your Turn" exercise in this chapter. Even if it eventually came to nothing, list the obstacles it faced as a vision. Who or what opposed it? Why?

_____

_____

_____

_____

_____

_____

Fortunately, a third choice is available to leaders: listen carefully to objections and assess their validity. If they contain an important truth or perspective, adapt the vision accordingly. In Richard's case, this adaptation meant limiting his idea for a student service to nonhealth issues. The Suicide Prevention Hotline was still free to do its thing completely independent from Richard's plan. With this change, Richard won widespread support for his idea, received university funding, and within a few months had the popular student service up and running.

BEING A LEADER OF ONESELF

Leadership is often understood to imply a parade of sorts, with the most important person at the front and the gang of followers close behind. In this version, the leader's primary focus is on taking his or her followers in the right direction (or at least keeping them in line), while the followers' main focus is on paying attention to the leader's signals and doing what he or she says.

As a helpful exercise in reconceptualizing the nature of leadership, imagine that the gang of followers is missing entirely. We have only the leader proceeding down the street alone. He or she must still make decisions about direction, purpose, pace, costume, behavior, and all the other matters that pertain to presenting oneself in public. In short, he or she must be his or her own leader. This somewhat arresting notion has been interpreted by some as the leadership version of a slightly altered Golden Rule: Do unto others as you would do unto yourself.

Spelled out more precisely, being a leader of oneself suggests at least five guidelines useful to leaders in all contexts:

1. Consider your limits as a leader and measure your resources carefully. A leader of oneself should not push past his or her limitations.
2. Watch where you step. A leader of oneself should avoid pitfalls for his or her own welfare as well as that of followers.
3. Find the best route. The inconvenience and delays occasioned by taking the wrong route are amplified only when others are following.
4. Know why you are marching. The leader of oneself can explain not only the route for the journey but also its purpose.
5. Know when you have arrived. The leader of oneself recognizes when the destination has been attained and does not push on incessantly as if the journey were its own reward.

GENERATING IDEAS

If you do not wake up each morning bursting with bright ideas for changing the world, don't conclude that you have no leadership potential. Like all of us, leaders have to work at the task of generating useful ideas. Consider two ways in which this work often takes place.

The Brainstorming Session

Some leaders hatch their best ideas and visions by bouncing questions, opinions, and other thoughts back and forth with others. In a student setting, such a brainstorming session may take place with friends in a dorm room or student lounge. In the business world, brainstorming is often the agenda for meetings. As a general rule, this free and vigorous expression of ideas works best when the group is no larger than eight or ten people. Larger groups tend to divide quickly into sides or, just as often, into a small contingent of arguers and a large number of mere spectators.

Guidelines for a productive brainstorming session are simple:

- Listen carefully to what others are saying.
- Express your ideas frankly and clearly.
- Resist the temptation to force early conclusions.
- Allow more than one idea to flourish.
- Base your arguments on ideas and circumstances, not on people and personalities.

Although all cultures have employed the brainstorming session in making some of history's most important decisions, this form of idea generation and testing has been particularly crucial to U. S. political development. Perhaps because a democracy by nature welcomes a variety of viewpoints, American national leaders have frequently used brainstorming sessions to find strategic solutions to difficult world problems. During the Cuban missile crisis of the mid-1960s, President John F. Kennedy assembled a discussion group made up not only of his political allies but also of those who objected to most of his positions. He told the group not to abide by any set agenda or rules or order. Instead, they were to speak openly and honestly about how they believed the United States should respond to the prospect of having Russian nuclear missile sites only 90 miles from its borders. President Kennedy took an additional step to make sure that this brainstorming activity was not restricted unnecessarily by his presence. He told the group that he would purposely be missing several meetings so that all opinions—especially those that might not be said to the president's face—could be aired and evaluated.

Fortunately, that no-holds-barred approach to idea generation produced a workable political plan and strategy that led to the dismantling of missile sites and a lessening in world tension.

In city government and student life, the town hall meeting is a popular variant on the brainstorming concept. All attendees have a right to speak up with questions, answers, facts, objections, criticisms, support, alternative ideas, and simple gut feelings.

Some leaders do not assemble all participants in a town hall or other room for a brainstorming session but instead visit them individually to understand their thoughts and perspectives. This is the common practice of many Fortune 500 corporate leaders. They schedule an extended series of meetings with individuals and small groups representing various stakeholders affected by a new vision or idea. In these meetings, the company leader and the leader's assistants ask probing questions, take careful notes, and listen intently to what their invitees have to say. Out of this information gathering come more useful and workable ideas—in effect, a practical vision.

YOUR TURN

Describe a brainstorming session in which you have participated. What helped group members talk freely about their ideas? What hindered their efforts to brainstorm?

_____

_____

_____

_____

_____

Flexibility and Leadership Skills

Leadership is much like the act of driving a car. In some conditions, the steering wheel must be gripped tightly and turned often. In other circumstances, the driver maintains a light hand on the wheel and may not turn at all for several miles at a time. No single leadership behavior can be used habitually and universally without reference to the human context. Max DePree, in *Leadership Is an Art*, compares leadership to the flexibility and freedom of a jazz musician finding interesting motifs that fit an underlying set of harmonies. Similarly, a leader "plays" a situation by paying attention to its basic themes and adapting his or her own actions (or improvisations) accordingly.

The Ten Classic Questions for Leaders

In the days of Plato and Aristotle, Greek schools sought to teach their future leaders not only how to speak and act but also how to think. Toward this end, Greek schools used one or more versions of the Classic Questions. These easy-to-use inquiries have been used ever since by leaders who want to think broadly and deeply about problems and situations. For at least 3,000 years, leaders have used such questions as a mental exercise designed to produce better, more informed ideas.

Here's how to use the Classic Questions to enrich your approach to generating ideas and visions. Define in advance some topic that you want to think intensely about. That topic—for example, "the war on terrorism"—gets inserted into the blank in each of the following questions. Read the question to yourself, think about your answers, then jot down what you consider your best thoughts or impressions before moving on to the next question. Not all questions, of course, will fit all topics. But most questions will yield some insight that, added up over the course of all 10 questions, will almost guarantee a more complete, in-depth set of ideas and overall vision for dealing with your chosen topic.

The Classic Questions

1. If _____ had to be divided into its most important parts or aspects, what would they be?
2. How did _____ come about or rise to concern?

3. Who cares most about _____? Why? Who cares least about _____? Why?

4. In order, what are the three most important facts about _____?

5. What information is not yet known about _____? How can such information be gained?

6. How does _____ compare in importance to other similar issues or matters? Why is it more or less important?

7. If _____ did not exist, how would the world or particular groups be affected? Why?

8. What are the three most powerful barriers or obstacles to resolving _____? Explain why each is powerful.

9. What feelings does _____ arouse in you? In others? Why?

10. If you had to explain _____ to a 10-year-old child, what would you say?

Notice that no one question in itself claims to deliver fresh ideas struck from the brow of Zeus. Rather, each question jogs the mind in a different way so that, by the end of the question routine, you possess many new ways to think about your topic. By definition, creative thought means stepping out of old mental ruts and clichés to find better, perhaps more original ways of thinking about problems and solutions. Such creative thinking is the fertile ground of vision for leadership.

INSIGHT 7

Ideas that make up a workable vision usually come from purposeful idea-seeking activity rather than from passive waiting for inspiration.

YOUR TURN

Choose a topic or idea that currently interests you. Insert it in each of the blanks for the Classic Questions, and jot down brief answers for each question that fits your chosen topic or idea.

_____

_____

_____

_____

_____

_____

THE PERSONAL RISKS OF EXPRESSING A VISION

Expressing a vision is very much like putting your hand on the steering wheel of a moving vehicle. On the one hand, you have control of where the vehicle goes and can influence its future course. You have status as the driver, and others look to you for their safety. On the other hand, you have responsibility in case the vehicle ends up in the ditch instead of at its intended destination. Your fame can quickly turn to infamy.

Ambition, excitement, and confidence may motivate you to sit in the driver's seat in the first place. But it often takes courage and alert senses to stay there.

Leadership expert Charles Handy put the matter well: "A belief in oneself is the only thing that gives an individual the self-confidence to step into the unknown and to persuade others to go where no one has gone before. But this has to be combined with a decent doubt, the humility to accept that one can be wrong on occasion, that others also have ideas, that listening is as important as talking."[4]

YOUR TURN

Jot down the personal pros and cons of a leadership role you have played in your school, home, civic, religious, or work life. What did you like about the role? What difficulties did you experience or worry about?

_____

_____

_____

_____

_____

In student and business organizations, leaders quickly learn that some kinds of visions have a better chance of success than others. Here is a general rule of thumb by which to assess your own leadership visions:

INSIGHT 8

A vision must depart significantly from the status quo (or else its ideas will be perceived as "me-too" thoughts rather than a leadership vision). But the vision must not go beyond the general limits of possibility as perceived by followers (because ideas perceived as impossible will be dismissed as crazy or wrongheaded).

Consider the situation of Rachel G. who following college graduation had the opportunity to play a leadership role as a manager in a large family business.

"It felt funny at first to have dozens of mature men and women looking to me for my ideas on how we could improve company productivity. Especially in my first weeks on the job, I was afraid that someone who knew more or had many years of experience with the company would shoot down my ideas and make me look foolish as a new leader. Luckily, I learned quickly that others didn't want to take over my job—they just wanted their input to be heard. When my vision for how things could be improved included or at least recognized that input, I usually had good support from my team. If an occasional one of my ideas was so far out as to be unworkable in the company, my people were loyal enough that they would tell me straight out what they thought. I don't feel so much at risk anymore as a leader because I see that the rest of the work team plays an important role in keeping me on the right track. They want the company to succeed as much as I do."

YOUR TURN

Tell about a time that a leader's idea seemed just too "far out" for you to accept and follow. What could the leader have done to bring you aboard with the idea?

_____

_____

_____

_____

_____

_____

LEADERSHIP AND GENDER

The road for women to full and equal recognition as leaders still runs uphill. In 2008, less than 10 percent of Fortune 1000 companies were headed by women, and virtually no Fortune 100 companies. Board memberships for women in Fortune 1000 companies was a mere 14 percent. To the extent that business schools are a training ground for leaders of the future, the prospects were not good for women: the majority of business schools hovered around a 2 to 1 imbalance between male and female MBA students in 2008.

Why? Certainly not because of objective measures of academic accomplishment and intelligence. Women score at equal levels or above men on standardized tests such as the SAT, GRE, and GMAT. Sociologists point to at least three forces that keep many women from rising in organizations to where their talent should take them.

1. *The force of tradition.* Since the Industrial Revolution, men have controlled the world of business. The phrase "captains of industry" reveals how thoroughly male our society considers its corporate leaders. Sadly, tradition takes on a life of its own, apart from any connection to logic or fairness. The "good old boy" network at upper corporate echelons is not a Hollywood myth. It exists in the form of well-established male leaders who look to people like themselves when making appointments to corporate boards and other leadership positions.

2. *Cultural misunderstanding of courage and power.* In the American family of legend (if not actuality), the father stands as the ultimate judge, provider, and protector for family members. (This stereotype continues to exist in spite of the fact that both parents are employed in more than half of American households and that the woman's pay in a traditional heterosexual union often exceeds the man's pay.) The patterns and expectations of leadership and dominance in the home carry over into the workplace. "Secretary" is a feminine job category, along with "nurse" and "elementary school teacher," to many unthinking people. By contrast, "physician," "pilot," "lawyer," "professor," and "mayor" are almost automatically judged to be male positions. Fighting these preconceptions is difficult, especially when they are confirmed in most television, magazine, and Internet entertainment. When it comes time to choose a leader in business or other organizations, it somehow "feels right" to many people when a man is chosen because that selection accords with all the cultural cues and prods that surround them. A woman, in their minds, might buckle under stress or find herself overwhelmed when facing tough decisions. (These prejudices are alive and well in spite of the evidence to the contrary from women who have successfully led companies and countries in our time.)

3. *The interruptive influence of childbearing and child-rearing.* In the past decade, some American corporations proclaimed that they had devised a "mommy track" for rising corporate women who wanted to take time off for motherhood or at least create sufficient flextime in their jobs for parenthood. For all the good press such programs brought to these companies, the harsh reality for most women was that "time off was time lost" in the competitive battle to climb the corporate ladder. In many cases, talented women took a year or more off from their corporate positions without any guarantee that they could return to their same rank and pay. Unlike most Scandinavian and European countries, no protections existed in law to enable a woman to bear and raise children without risking the loss of her job, or at least the inability to return to the place she left in the company hierarchy. For many women who attempted to "do it all" by raising children and also competing successfully as corporate leaders, the result was too often mental and physical exhaustion. One expert coined the term "the second shift" for executive women who were in fact putting in almost twice the hours of labor per week as their male counterparts, when parenting and spousal duties were added to work responsibilities.

Even though women continue to enter the workforce in larger numbers each year (often in response to a worsening economy and the need for families to pay their bills), the battle for gender equality is far from won. Women tend to take lower-paying and lower-responsibility positions, regardless of their skill levels compared to men. (For example, what gender comes to mind when you think of a "temp"?)

An important message in this book is that leadership is and should be gender-blind. No tip or technique discussed in these pages is intended or assumed to be more appropriate for one gender over the other. Perhaps because this book was written by a man and a woman, we have been especially careful not to tilt examples, principles, or precepts toward one gender when it comes to developing leadership abilities.

VISIONARY ACTIONS

So far we have discussed leadership vision expressed in words: Richard's plan for student services, President Kennedy's approach to the Cuban missile crisis, and Rachel's leadership ideas in a corporate setting. But leaders frequently find that a visionary action—some highly visible act, "happening," or performance—speaks louder and more memorably than a host of visionary words.

Take, for example, the leadership choice facing Arthur Houghton Jr., CEO of Corning Glass, when he had to announce to the world in the mid-1900s that Corning no longer wanted to be thought of as a specialized "art glass" and crystal crafter but instead as an industrial giant producing common cookware and glass-based manufacturing materials. Houghton could have written a typical speech expressing his new vision for the direction of the company. Instead, he chose a visionary action to express his point. In full view of invited cameras, reporters, stockholders, employees, and the general public, Houghton grabbed a lead pipe and summarily smashed more than $100,000 worth of fine crystal. No one could mistake his point: Corning was out of the crystal business.

YOUR TURN

Describe a time when you showed your vision, opinion, or point of view by an action rather than by words. (Even slamming the door can be an expression of perspective.) Explain why you chose this action rather than words to make your point. What was the result?

_____

_____

_____

_____

_____

_____

_____

Visionary actions are particularly powerful when a leader wants to communicate a clear, sharp break with past practices. For example, Scott McNealy, president of Sun Microsystems, wanted to demonstrate to the workforce that his leadership would be different in tone, spirit, and manner from that of other corporate presidents. With thousands of his workers assembled in an amphitheater for a company convention, McNealy came bumping and roaring down the aisle to the stage on a Harley motorcycle. Workers buzzed about his surprising entrance for months after the meeting. He got their attention for a change in leadership style in a way that no speech could have achieved.

In the context of student life, visionary actions also have a remarkable history for communicating new departures and ideas. In the 1960s, students simply sat down in the offices and hallways of administrators as a way of showing their power, purpose, and solidarity. A student perched in an old-growth redwood tree for several weeks in Northern California as a visionary protest against logging practices there. On a smaller scale, a candidate for office in the student government of a Texas college showed up at a student rally wearing a Superman suit. He wanted to announce loud and clear—and largely without words—that he was the candidate capable of bold programs and reforms.

Such visionary actions are particularly necessary, it seems, when words alone are overlooked or undervalued. Jack Welch, CEO of General Electric, 1981–2001, referred to his many corporate reforms in the action metaphor of cleaning out an old house: "How would you like to move from a house after 112 years? Think of what would be in the closets and the attic—those shoes that you'll wear to paint next spring, even though you know you'll never paint again. We've got 112 years of closets and attics in this company. We want to flush them out to start with a brand-new house with empty closets, to begin the whole game again."[5]

INSIGHT 9

What you do—visibly and with conviction—speaks at least as loudly as what you say as a leader.

LEADING ON THE SMALL STAGE

It's safe to say that most readers of this book (as well as the authors) do not consider themselves the leadership peers of Arthur Houghton at Corning Glass, Scott McNealy at Sun Microsystems, or Jack Welch when he was at General Electric. The great majority of us exercise leadership skills on a smaller stage. But the lessons learned from leadership giants can easily be translated to our leadership of work groups, clubs, civic organizations, and even the smallest committees. Like Arthur Houghton, we can use a dramatic gesture of some kind to make our point in a powerful way. Like Scott McNealy, we can exceed and surprise the expectations of others by imaginative and even humorous acts. Like Jack Welch, we can break out of jargon and bureaucratic language to express ourselves clearly and creatively.

Instrument for Reflection and Discussion

"WHAT MOTIVATES YOU TO LEAD?"

Admittedly, different situations call out different motives for an individual's rise to leadership. For example, the situation of an army unit backed into a corner by hostile enemies may cause one individual to rise to leadership, rally the troops, and save the day. As another example, a single mother faced with crushing financial and parenting responsibilities may find the energy and courage to lead a support group of individuals in similar circumstances.

This instrument asks you to call to mind many of your life experiences, thoughts, and feelings to determine in a general way what kinds of forces motivate you to rise to leadership.

Directions: *Take a few quiet moments to think through your school and work life to date. In particular, think about aspects of those experiences that went well for you and those that did not go so well. Recall times when you felt others looked up to you and joined your cause as well as times when you felt that you were "going it alone" without support from others. After these moments of reflection, circle the letters (as many as you wish) of those choices offered in the following that come closest to describing in general the kinds of circumstances and feelings that are influential in motivating you to rise to a leadership role:*

"I am usually motivated to take on a leadership role when":

a. I see a situation I care about going downhill because no one else is stepping up to help.

b. I see someone else taking the wrong path—a path that I believe will lead to certain disaster for a project or plan I care about.

c. I strongly believe in an idea and want to do everything I can to advance it.

d. I am surrounded by other gung ho individuals who are also willing to be leaders rather than followers.

e. I sense that others will suffer or be disadvantaged in some way unless I act as a leader.

f. I conclude that the approaches suggested by others aren't very good and that my approach(es) will work better.

g. I recognize that playing a leadership role will pay me dividends in the long run, perhaps as a resume builder or entrance point to a career opportunity.

h. I feel pressured by others who know my history and abilities to take on a leadership position.

i. I am swayed to take a leadership role by the earnest appeals and compliments of others.

j. I know that my bosses expect me to take on a leadership role and will be disappointed if I don't.

k. I feel it will simply be more energizing and fun to be "part of the action" as a leader instead of at the margins as a follower.

l. I am curious about how far a plan, idea, or issue can be taken if I take on a leadership role in its promotion.

m. I am convinced that great rewards will be forthcoming, particularly to those who led the process, from the success of a project or plan.

n. I know my duties are specifically described and will not turn into an overly long or burdensome commitment.

o. I will be working with people I enjoy and who enjoy me.

p. I can discover the "inside story" and full facts only by participating at the highest level as a leader.

q. I feel it is "my turn" to lead after a prolonged period of patient followership of others.

r. I recognize that there is no one else qualified to take on the role of leader except me.

s. I have a history of successful leadership roles and want to maintain that track record.

t. I know I have the skill set(s) to make the process or project efficient and effective rather than disorganized and discouraging.

DRAWING CONCLUSIONS:

From the choices you have made, you have identified important aspects of your own motivations as a leader. In the following space, use these circled choices to sum up "what makes you tick" as a motivated leader: _____
_____
_____.

Now use your conclusions to compare and contrast your motivations with others in your group. What primary differences do you note between your base of motivations and those of others? _____
_____
_____.

Summing Up

Vision isn't the possession of the blessed or the special. It is available as a powerful but common skill to anyone who wants to succeed as a leader. Vision comes not only from the leader's own thoughts and imagination but also from the input of others. Brainstorming and the use of the Classic Questions can stimulate a leader's ability to form an insightful vision. In many circumstances, the expression of that vision by actions proves more memorable than by words alone. Visionary leadership can prove challenging to people, including many women, who have been unjustly excluded from consideration for top positions. In these cases, fairness and an appreciation for talent require that society remove prejudicial barriers to leadership roles.

4

Leadership by Listening

GOALS

- grasp the important role of listening in leadership
- learn better ways to listen
- apply what you learn from listening to the task of making better leadership decisions

Let's assume that you are not the CEO of a major corporation and don't have such an individual as a close acquaintance. (Most of us don't!) You're entirely the right person to answer the following question.

YOUR TURN

What do you think is the most common activity for such a corporate leader during an average workday? Please take a moment to jot down your answer to this question.

_____

_____

_____

_____

_____

We posed this same question to about 100 undergraduate students at three California universities. Their answers clustered around four main areas:

- "giving speeches"
- "telling subordinates what to do"
- "leading meetings with division or department heads"
- "hobnobbing with other corporate leaders and politicians"

Good guesses but no cigar. In fact, studies of actual CEO activity during the business day shows that—surprisingly—these leaders spend well over half their time *listening* to others. In interviews, they listen to what job candidates say; in meetings, they listen to reports and discussion; in conference calls, they listen to what Wall Street is saying about their company.

INSIGHT 10

Actual leaders spend most of their time listening to others.

That is a leadership insight worth contemplating. As a student body president in New York put it: "Listening is like looking down a slope before you begin to ski and continuing to look ahead as you ski. You can plan in advance where to go fast, where to slow down, what to avoid, and what to make use of and enjoy." Using her analogy, the opposite of leadership listening is painful to think about: skiing straight into trees, coming upon icy patches without warning, and missing the fun of powder and moguls.

YOUR TURN

Describe a time when you or an acquaintance took action before listening thoroughly. What was the result? How could that result have been avoided?

_____

_____

_____

_____

_____

THE ART OF LEADERSHIP LISTENING

Listening is more than hearing. The latter is simply the physical act of receiving sound waves through your auditory nerves. Wherever you find yourself at this moment, you are probably conscious of hearing certain sounds—an automobile, the wind in the trees, the whine of a siren, a door closing in the library, voices from others. These are the sounds that surround us and to which we usually give little attention.

But what have you been *listening* to in the past hour? If a teacher was speaking, were you listening or merely hearing? If a radio or TV was turned on, did it have your full listening attention or was it just part of the background sound that surrounds you?

YOUR TURN

Describe three sound sensations in your present environment that you can hear but have not been listening to (for example, the hum of a computer or air conditioner). Then describe some sound, perhaps someone's voice, that you have listened to, not merely heard. Based on your examples, how would you describe the difference between hearing and listening?

_____

_____

_____

_____

_____

Listening usually takes one of three forms: passive, attentive, or empathetic. Each requires increasingly more effort and concentration on our part—and yields increasingly more advantage for effective leadership.

Passive Listening

This form of listening occurs when we turn half an ear to background sound, such as music, while pursuing another, more involving activity, such as reading. We know that a song is playing in the background, but we are not actively attending to its melody or lyrics. It is not uncommon for students to fall into this passive form of listening during a professor's lecture. Like music, "the voice" drones on in the classroom but is mere background sound to the students' own thoughts about a coming sports event, a date, or a personal worry of some kind. Businesspeople have the same experience at some meetings, where the same voices seem to be saying the same things they have heard many times before. As Jerry Seinfeld would say, "Yada yada yada."

YOUR TURN

Describe one or more specific occasions when you find it tempting to listen passively. Explain why you find it difficult to listen more attentively on these occasions.

_____

_____

_____

_____

_____

_____

_____

INSIGHT 11

Without our conscious effort, much that we should be listening to will be missed.

Certain stimuli can yank us out of passive listening to the next stage—attentive listening. If in the middle of a droning lecture, a professor says "Remember this for the test," we exit our sleepy realm of passive listening and listen with focus, at least for a minute or two. If the CD player begins to skip tracks on the background music we've been playing, we listen up and take note of the problem. If at a boring meeting the boss suddenly says, "What do you think, Frank?"—and your name is Frank—listening quickly turns from passive to attentive.

Attentive Listening

In this form of listening, we are listening *for* something: listening for the whistle of the teakettle, listening for the solution to a math problem, listening for the question we will have to answer, and so forth. One test for attentive listening is whether we can name what we are listening for. If we can, we are listening at the attentive stage.

Students listen attentively when they are paying attention to what an instructor or a fellow student is saying; when they are trying to figure out the words being sung by a vocal artist; when they are determining what may be wrong with a car, based on its strange noises; and when they are listening for boarding instructions at an airport. Similarly, business professionals listen attentively when the accounting department calls them with questions about business travel expenses and when the TV anchorperson begins a news story about impending layoffs in their industry. If the topic has your attention, you're at the attentive stage of listening.

YOUR TURN

Describe some sound source to which you have listened attentively at some time during the past hour. What was it about that source that led you to listen attentively?

_____

_____

_____

_____

_____

_____

INSIGHT 12

Attentive listening can help a leader pick out key items of information useful for decision making.

Empathetic Listening

The final stage of listening—and certainly the most difficult and potentially fulfilling—occurs when we are listening *with* rather than listening *for*. For example, in a heart-to-heart conversation with a friend about a recent romantic breakup, we are not listening for particular instructions or a specific set of words but instead are listening with our emotions engaged. This is empathetic listening, the stage of listening most useful for leadership purposes.

Empathetic listening occurs when we make an effort to understand the speaker's feelings as well as the words. We are attuned to the unspoken messages communicated by pauses, sighs, laughs, facial expressions, and gestures.

Listening with the speaker's emotions, hopes, desires, perceptions, points of view, values, and so forth does not mean that you must agree with those factors. Empathetic listening simply means that you are engaged in the effort to hear the whole message, rational and emotional, without judging it or censoring it in midstream.

Here's an extended example of empathetic listening as experienced by a student nurse and her chief nurse supervisor. Chief Nurse Higgins arrives on her assigned hospital floor at 7 A.M. The first person she encounters is student nurse Linda, who looks frazzled, exhausted, and upset. Before Nurse Higgins can even say "good morning," Linda blurts out the following:

"What a night! Two of our staff didn't show up for work, we had three emergencies, and both Mr. Baxter and Ms. Cox had terrible problems. In fact, I thought we would lose Ms. Cox when she began hemorrhaging again, but we saved her. And then you wanted me to complete the monthly status report in my free time, which I did, but I had to begin my shift two hours early to get it done and it was almost impossible to fit it in. If I never have another night like this last one, it will be too soon."

If Chief Nurse Higgins had been listening passively to Linda's words, she would probably reply, "Uh-huh. We'll catch up later." We have all had people "blow us off" by such passive listening. We cannot help but feel hurt and angered by their lack of concern for what we are trying to express.

If Chief Nurse Higgins had been listening attentively to Linda's words, however, she would probably reply, "That's good news about Baxter and Cox. You can leave your status report on my desk before you leave today." In other words, attentive listening lets Chief Nurse Higgins listen only for key phrases that resolve particular problems she faces: Are Baxter and Cox stable? Is the report completed? To such attentive listening, the student nurse would probably feel like screaming, "Aren't you listening to me?" When people miss the main message we think we're sending and choose bits and pieces of it for their attention, we feel as ignored and undervalued as when we are treated simply as background sound.

The point for leaders is obvious: no leader lasts long by ignoring and undervaluing his or her followers. *The way a leader listens* tells followers where they stand more convincingly than the way a leader speaks.

YOUR TURN

Although you may protect actual names as you wish, tell about an experience in which you listened empathetically rather than just attentively. Did the way you listened have a positive, negative, or neutral effect on the speaker? Please explain your answer.

_____

_____

_____

_____

_____

_____

If Chief Nurse Higgins had been listening empathetically to her student nurse, she would have heard Linda trying to say several more subtle messages:

"I deserve some praise for extraordinary effort last night under frightening conditions."
"You were unreasonable to ask me to complete the status report."
"I need help keeping this job without burning out."

By listening empathetically, Chief Nurse Higgins gives herself a chance to respond to the deeper meanings of Linda's words and thereby to increase Linda's job satisfaction, her loyalty to Chief Nurse Higgins, and her effectiveness with patients.

INSIGHT 13

Empathetic listening involves an effort on our part to hear the whole message, including its emotional content.

WHY LEADERS OFTEN FAIL TO LISTEN

Telling leaders that they should listen empathetically doesn't necessarily make it happen. Powerful barriers are at work that cause many leaders to become worse and worse at listening as they rise in the corporate hierarchy. Here are six of these barriers.

Lack of Time

As a leader deals with an ever-increasing supply of information, the availability of time to listen seems to decrease. Some individuals require more time than others when they are speaking to you. If you appear to be impatient, they will walk away in frustration or find several ways to repeat their message until you "get it." Some people don't hesitate to monopolize your listening time. Unless you make tactful efforts to end the conversation, you could literally be listening all day.

By contrast, there are others with whom you work or live that you should listen to with undivided attention. Remember, if you do not listen to them, they will find someone who will. If employees feel their supervisor won't listen to them, they will find other employees or union representatives or administrators who will. If students feel a professor doesn't listen to them, they will seek out the ear of a dean. If customers feel a supplier isn't listening, they will take their business to a competitor.

Conditioning

Over time, many of us may have trained ourselves to tune out messages with which we do not agree. Life, we may reason, seems to roll along much more smoothly when we simply "change channels" instead of confronting upsetting news. We may carry such conditioning directly into our listening habits with others.

Snap Judgments

If we make immediate evaluations and judgments about the worth of what we are listening to, it is unlikely that we will ever hear the whole message. We may mentally reject what the speaker is saying from the outset and then take an "attention vacation" until the individual is done speaking. By delaying judgment, we give ourselves a chance to receive information that may be in our best interests.

Emotional Curtains

Any dominant emotion we are experiencing—frustration, anger, elation, fear—can block messages from reaching our attention or empathy. Leaders must learn to turn down emotions when they're trying to listen.

Lack of Training

Most of us have spent hundreds of hours in classes devoted to writing. In one form or another, we've also practiced speaking in many circumstances and with groups of various sizes. But even though we spend most of our formal education supposedly listening to instructors, the fact remains that few of us have had any training in listening skills. For many readers, this chapter may be the first time the importance and art of listening have been explained. Leaders can be taught to listen more effectively—and their success in such lessons determines in large part their eventual leadership success.

Failure to Concentrate

Look around the room at the next class or meeting you attend. Note how many participants sit sprawled in their chairs, their eyes averted from the speaker, their faces in an apparent apathetic daze, or focused on their cell phone screen for their latest

---

YOUR TURN

Describe two or more key reasons why on some occasions you have not listened as well as you should have. You can choose from the reasons discussed earlier or add reasons of your own.

_____

_____

_____

_____

_____

text message. These participants have decided not to work at the task of listening. They have made a choice that no leader can afford to make.

EMOTIONAL INTELLIGENCE AND LEADERSHIP

In a world where all problems could be solved by rational analysis and action, leadership training would consist of nothing more than "book smarts"—that is, the kind of intelligence that solves math problems, remembers the names of the rivers of Russia, and can tell you when and why the Magna Carta was signed.

It will come as no surprise that many, if not most, business problems are not resolved by the application of this kind of intelligence alone. In addition, leaders are characterized by a high degree of "emotional intelligence" or EQ. Here's an example of EQ from the world of city politics:

> "A member of the city council was so angry that raises had been denied for council members that he marched into the Mayor's office and swore directly into her face. Most of thought that the Mayor would shout back; she certainly had good logical reasons for not giving the council members their raises. But instead she just raised her hand to silence the screaming guy and walked out of the room, leaving him standing there looking foolish and with no one to berate."

In this case, the Mayor applied EQ—also known as wisdom, maturity, perspective, and control—to a problem that probably would have only become worse by the application of logic. Even if her reasons for refusing the raise were completely defensible from a rational perspective, she recognized that the council member was in no position to hear what she had to say, much less think about it. Therefore, she exercised EQ, allowing some time and distance between her and the apoplectic council member. In fact, a day later when he had calmed down they had an extended and relatively restrained conversation about the whole matter of raises.

We learn EQ in school as surely as we learn to be rational thinkers. Here are three common ways in which our school experiences have enhanced our EQ:

- Reading novels, short stories, and in-depth history shows us what is going on in the hearts as well as the heads of people, fictional or real.
- Observing how our classmates interact with one another and seeing how others (including instructors) handle stressful situations teach us much about the value of EQ. We make judgments about who dealt with problems wisely and who "let it get to them" as evidenced by bitterness, anger, and the impulse for revenge.
- Testing alternative ways of relating to others, including friends and acquaintances, provides a social laboratory of sorts in which we each learn what works and doesn't work in relating to others. Sometimes we "learn the hard way" by saying or doing entirely the wrong thing for the situation at hand. In these circumstances, our EQ probably jumps upward a few points—we learn better ways to cope with difficult issues or personalities.

INSIGHT 14

Leaders can point to many reasons why they aren't good listeners, but none of these reasons excuses them from the obligation and opportunity to listen.

KEYS TO IMPROVED LISTENING

Leaders and leaders-in-training can undertake personal practice in better listening by committing to four keys for improvement.

1. *Create a "meaning road map" as you listen.* Where is the speaker coming from? Where is she headed in the conversation? What unexpected detours take place and why? What potholes does the speaker seem to experience on the road? By tracking a conversation this way, a leader can condense a flood of words into a clear, understandable message. By mentally accompanying the speaker on this journey of words, the leader can aid conversation by helping the speaker over the rough spots and by pointing out shortcuts that the speaker may not have seen.

2. *Appreciate the speaker's meaning for the words he or she chooses.* Words have different meanings for different people. For example, does the speaker share your meaning of the word *responsibility* in telling you, "I want more responsibility here, and I don't want people looking over my shoulder when I take a break or decide to work at home." In this context, *responsibility* to the speaker apparently means freedom from supervision. For successful communication, make sure you and the speaker share the same meanings for key words. In this case, the listener might respond, "I hear you saying that you want to be accountable for your own breaks and work schedule." By shifting the language in this way, the listener has removed the misused word *responsibility* from the conversation and has substituted words that get to the heart of the matter.

3. *Observe nonverbal communication while you listen.* Hand gestures, drumming fingers, tapping toes, voice inflections, worried glances, facial expressions, perspiration, cracking knuckles, voice intensity, and posture are some of the nonverbal messages that tell volumes about what a speaker is trying to communicate. If you sense strong but unspoken feelings on the part of the speaker, you can call attention to them: "You obviously have strong feelings about this. Tell me why."

4. *Listen with an open mind.* We all carry biases into communication experiences with others. For example, a boss may assume that an employee who wants to talk about a flexible work schedule is in fact trying to do less work. A professor listening to a student's inquiry about the reasons for a low semester grade may assume that the student dislikes and mistrusts the professor. The student in this situation may assume that the professor resents the grade inquiry and will stubbornly resist making a grade change. Although these factors may at times be true, often they are not true. Unfortunately, by believing them *always* to be the case, the people involved virtually guarantee that they *will* turn out to be

true. Better by far to approach listening experiences with your mind open to whatever the moment presents.

5. *Select, if possible, the right time and place for meaningful listening.* All of the advice given up to this point can't help a leader who attempts to listen at the wrong time ("I've got a class in three minutes!") or the wrong place ("This restaurant is really noisy and doesn't give us much privacy, but go ahead and talk."). If listening is important, it deserves careful placement in our day. Postponing a conversation temporarily for a better time and place is almost always taken by the speaker as a sign that the listener truly cares about the conversation and wants to engage in its issues fully.

YOUR TURN

Which of the keys for improved listening provided earlier seem most useful for your own practice in better listening? Choose as many as you wish from the list and/or add techniques of your own.

_____

_____

_____

_____

_____

_____

INSIGHT 15

Listening, like most other skills, can be improved through training and practice.

WHAT LEADERS GAIN BY IMPROVED LISTENING

Good listening is not a matter of politeness or "polish" for leaders—something akin to good table manners. Instead, good listening is a strategic advantage that gives competitive edge to leaders at all levels. Here's how:

First, leaders who listen well end up knowing more than others. They have developed the skill to be quiet and receive information that they may want to filter out, but should not. In the case of the *Challenger* disaster, a leader decided not to "hear" the message of a faulty O-ring problem. In the case of Pearl Harbor, the Navy admirals in charge decided not to attend to rumors and reports of an impending attack. A commitment to listening gives a leader full information on which to base decisions.

Second, leaders who listen well build loyalty and morale. Listening is a way of expressing respect and caring which, in turn, lead to school and work relationships that are more cooperative, productive, and downright fun.

Finally, leaders who listen well respond successfully to change and crisis. In late-late-night movies, a wilderness guide often puts his or her ear to the ground to listen for signs of approaching horses (buffalo, reindeer, kangaroos, or what have you). A good leader has his or her ear to the ground for signs of change and crisis. For example, Michael Dell, CEO of Dell Computer, spends at least as much energy listening to what people do not like about his company as to what they love about it. "In this business," Dell says, "there are two kinds of people: the quick and the dead."[6] Listening carefully for signs of market changes, financial shifts, customer preferences, and new business opportunities has given Dell an edge in remaining among the "quick" in the computer industry.

YOUR TURN

Describe a time when good listening gave you an advantage.

_____

_____

_____

_____

_____

INSIGHT 16

Leaders have much to gain for themselves and their organizations by learning to listen well.

Instrument for Reflection and Discussion

"WHY DO LEADERS SOMETIMES FAIL?"

In the following instrument, a wide variety of reasons are provided for why leaders at all levels (large and small stages) sometimes fail to achieve their own goals and those of the people they purport to lead.

Directions: *From among the twenty "failure factors" offered here, identify the five, in order of priority from most common (1) to less common (5), that you believe are most responsible for leadership failure.*

__ Flaws in personal character

__ Uncontrollable turn of events

__ Challenges from other leaders

__ Loss of energy and commitment to the cause

__ Poor strategic moves that alienate supporters

__ Inability to build a wide base of supporters

__ Lack of charisma and inspiration in leading others

__ Rumors (true or not) that undercut the leader's credibility and influence

__ Poor choices in the leader's association with questionable individuals or groups

__ Aspects of the leader's personal life that are not approved by supporters

__ Fanaticism about the cause, driving more level heads away

__ Illegal acts that remove the leader from power

__ High-handed tactics that make the leader appear brutal and uncaring

__ Failure to solicit input from others, resulting in a "know-it-all" reputation for the leader

__ Personality problems (such as insincerity, inappropriate sense of humor, or brusque interpersonal style) that reduce the leader's popularity

__ Poor communication abilities in public presentations, debates, and media appearances

__ Physical unattractiveness

__ A hit-and-miss track record, making people doubt the leader's competence

__ Less-than-admirable personal habits, including overreliance on alcohol or other substances, illicit sexual connections, and slovenly personal hygiene and dress

DRAWING CONCLUSION

Review the five factors you have selected as key components in leadership failure. Do your choices have anything in common? Prior to discussing your conclusions with your group, reflect on what you have observed to be the primary destructive forces at work in bringing down leaders. Call to mind and be prepared to discuss individual leaders who have been damaged by the problems you have circled.

Reflection comments: _____
_____
_____
_____.

Summing Up

Leaders can point to many reasons why they don't listen well: lack of time, conditioning, distraction, emotions, snap judgments, lack of training, and other factors. But all excuses aside, leaders must understand their own tendencies with regard to passive, attentive, and empathetic listening. By practicing such techniques as road mapping, key term definition, interpretation of nonverbal communication, keeping an open mind, and selecting appropriate times and places for listening, leaders attain several benefits: greater knowledge for decision making, enhanced loyalty and motivation among followers, and a vital early warning system in times of change and crisis.

5

Leadership by Building Relationships and Teams

GOALS

- understand that successful leadership always relies on strong relationships with team members
- learn new techniques for establishing relationships with team members
- develop skills in creating and leading effective teams

It's a truism that a well-led team depends upon good interpersonal relationships among team members. We can all think of our favorite members from teams we've served on or companies we've worked for. These are the people who can't wait to see you again, have their act together, and remember that your cat had a skin rash. How is she doing? No interpersonal relationship problems here!

But focusing only on these great relationships with exemplary team members is like "picking the low-hanging fruit." Your success as a leader, and the success of your organization, usually depends on stretching for relationships with those individuals who don't make work life easy for you and could care less about your cat. What follows in this chapter are tips for building productive relationships with these difficult team members.

SET ASIDE THE EASY ANSWERS

Beware of anyone who wants to whisper into your ear "the secret" of relating to difficult team members. Each person (as you know too well) is highly individualistic, even quirky. There's no magic phrase or single relationship formula for "difficult" people. However, you can prepare yourself and your organization for increased success with difficult individuals by thinking through the various obstacles that get in the way of your intended relationship with them. By understanding difficult team members more deeply, you can adapt to them more successfully and less stressfully. In short, you can be a skilled leader.

YOUR TURN

Omitting names, describe difficulties you have faced in working with a particular team member. How do you explain those difficulties?

_____

_____

_____

_____

_____

_____

INSIGHT 17

No leader can expect "smooth sailing" with all team members. Learning to work well with more difficult members is an important part of leadership development.

WHY DO CERTAIN TYPES OF PEOPLE BUG YOU?

Over the course of many experiences in school or work organizations, you will inevitably find yourself in an "oil-and-water" situation with some team members. Your personality type simply may not mix well with that of the difficult person.

A powerful key to dealing with these team members lies in recognizing how their personalities differ from your own. In 1921, the Swiss psychologist and philosopher Carl Jung proposed his theory of personality types. In later years, his theories have been championed by Katharine Briggs and Isabel Briggs Myers in the famous MBTI (Myers-Briggs Type Indicator®), a personality assessment administered in many MBA programs and other venues. This validated instrument helps people identify their personality tendencies and recognize how those tendencies may conflict with the quite different personalities of other people. In Chapter 2, you participated in an assessment similar to the MBTI. Look back at your results on that assessment.

For our purposes, the point is simple: "difficulty" in dealing with a client may largely be in the eye of the beholder. To bring this point home to your own business experience, think about the following four dimensions of personality described by Jung. Try to discover in these personality descriptions your own tendencies and habits of mind. Your results from Chapter 2 should be fresh in mind as you read on.

Member versus Self

Are you a Member, who values the company of others, seeks consensus in decisions, prefers to work in groups, and cares about belonging and popularity? Or, at the other end of the spectrum, are you a Self, who prefers to accomplish tasks alone, resists commonly held opinions and groupthink, and measures success by personal standards rather than group standards? (None of us is a "pure type"; try to place yourself somewhere on the continuum between Member and Self.)

Now imagine that you are working with a team member who has diametrically opposed personality tendencies to your own in this category. When a strong Self (you, let's say) works with a strong Member, obvious points of difficulty may arise. The Self will expect independent thinking and individual decision making: "Why can't you make the decision?" The Member, on the other hand, will need to consult others, be assured of the support of the group, and believe that the decision is not only right but popular: "Well, let me get back to you on this. Can we reschedule for tomorrow?"

YOUR TURN

What do you believe a Member should do in preparation for a meeting with a Self and vice versa?

_____

_____

_____

_____

_____

Planner versus Juggler

In the next dimension of personality, are you a Planner, who has a place for everything and everything in its place; who values organization and feels helpless without it; and who deals with change by making schedules, assigning tasks, and monitoring activities? Or are you a Juggler, who thrives on having many balls in the air at the same time, who finds unexpected developments and emergencies somewhat energizing and challenging, and who deals with change by coping moment to moment with circumstances and improvising solutions as necessary? Again, place yourself somewhere on the Planner–Juggler continuum.

You can foresee the train wreck that often occurs when a strong Planner tries to relate to a strong Juggler. The Planner wants to meet on time, finish business within an expected number of minutes, and button up all details in a timely manner. But if the team member is a strong Juggler, there is no such thing as a "certain amount of time" on the schedule or orderly processes for work. Business life is a rush of *maybes, in a few days, it depends,* and *get back to us.* The Juggler can drive the Planner nuts, and vice versa.

YOUR TURN

What do you believe a Planner should do in preparation for a meeting with a Juggler and vice versa?

_____

_____

_____

_____

Empathizer versus Thinker

In the next dimension of personality, are you an Empathizer, who makes decisions based on how you and others feel; who values friendship, loyalty, and camaraderie in the workplace; and who thinks first about who will be happy and who will be upset or angry when dealing with work situations? Or are you a Thinker, who cares most about logic and accuracy of information, who focuses on figuring out underlying causes and future effects, and who would rather be right than popular? Place yourself somewhere on the Empathizer–Thinker continuum.

When a strong Thinker sits down with a strong Empathizer, the two people may tend to "talk past" each other. The Thinker will spend energy setting forth logical positions and items of information, assuming that such material will lead the other team member to a speedy decision. But if that other member is a strong Empathizer, his or her energies in conversation will be devoted to emotional expression and self-testing: How do I really feel about what I'm hearing? How will others feel? How do I feel about the person I'm working with and about the atmosphere in the organization? What vibes am I getting? The Thinker may be frustrated by the

Empathizer's supposed "ignorance" and inability to follow a logical train of thought. The Empathizer may breathe a sigh of relief when leaving the Thinker's workplace—good riddance to that cold person and that organization too!

YOUR TURN

What do you believe an Empathizer should do in preparation for a meeting with a Thinker and vice versa?

_____

_____

_____

_____

_____

Closer versus Researcher

In the final dimension of personality, are you a Closer, who thinks that "we've talked long enough and it's time to act," who feels impatient when others want to contribute more and more information, and who wants to end one task or assignment as soon as possible to move on to new challenges? Or are you a Researcher, who welcomes new information and postpones final decision making as long as possible, who feels that quick action is probably foolhardy, and who finds excitement in the continual search for reliable information? Place yourself somewhere on the Closer–Researcher continuum.

For obvious reasons, the business world has large populations of both Closers and Researchers. "Look, let's just get this done!" the Closer seems to say. "Don't rush me," the Researcher seems to reply—and all the while tempers may be heating up on both sides.

YOUR TURN

What do you believe a Closer should do in preparation for a meeting with a Researcher and vice versa?

_____

_____

_____

_____

_____

INSIGHT 18

Leaders can build better relationships with team members by planning in advance for personality differences.

MAKING LEADERSHIP SENSE OUT OF PERSONALITY DIFFERENCES

What lessons can be learned from personality differences for the purpose of working well with a difficult team member? First, recognize that your personality is part of the equation causing the difficulty. Don't put all the blame on the team member. Second, approach any meeting with the team member with the expectation that your personality may grind a bit against that of the other person. Listen for these points of conflict, and make adjustments to relieve them. (For example, a Planner can have several backup ways to present information to an impatient Juggler, a Closer can try to understand the additional information needs of a Researcher, and a Thinker can bend to see things from the more emotional perspective of an Empathizer.)

Finally, become a personality detective in your organization. Learn to spot a Juggler, for example, by the way he or she fidgets in the chair and skips quickly from topic to topic. Recognize the Member or Empathizer by his or her conversational references to family and friends, personal feelings, and the ups and downs of his or her day. Spot the Planner, of course, by his or her reliance on schedules and agendas, his or her insistence on orderly procedures, and his or her eagerness to tell you about big-picture thinking. Then use the information gained from your detective work to help you manage your own leadership style and interpersonal relations.

Although you cannot (and should not) change your personality like a chameleon to match the personality of each team member you encounter, you can *understand* the root causes of a difficult relationship and make whatever adjustments you can to alleviate the stress points. You have everything to gain and nothing to lose as a leader by making the best of a difficult situation. "A few of my team members continue to be difficult for me to work with," a Washington, D.C., bank officer says, "but now I know why. And that has made all the difference."

INSIGHT 19

A leader does not have to change his or her personality to adapt to the needs of individual team members. Adjusting to someone else's needs does not mean denying one's own individuality.

USING NONVERBAL SIGNALS TO REVOLUTIONIZE YOUR LEADERSHIP RELATIONSHIPS

Team member returning from team meeting, reporting to her friend:

FRIEND: So what did your team leader say about missing the deadline for your part of the report?

TEAM MEMBER: The usual, but he looked really serious this time. I guess I'd better do something.

As leaders, we all trust our words too much to carry our messages to others. We think about "what we want to say," then assume that pronouncing those words will convey our thoughts and urgency to the listener. Rarely do we think about the more subtle but extremely powerful messages being sent by our eyes, faces, hands, posture, and other key aspects of nonverbal communication.

This is our mistake as leaders. In fact, more than 60 percent of the total communication passed from one person to another comes from nonverbal signals rather than the words themselves. You can test this assertion in an easy way: form an "O" by joining your thumb to your pointer finger. Ask someone else to do likewise. Then instruct the person: "Please put this 'O' on your chin." But as you say these words, put your own "O" on your cheek, not your chin. Where will the other person tend to put the "O" (as did up to 80 percent of people in group trials of this simple experiment)? You guessed it: on their *cheek* (as they saw you do) rather than on their *chin* (as they heard you say).

Put another way, many of your group members may be walking away from their meetings with you with your nonverbal message more in mind than the specific words you said. Before blaming them for ignoring or misunderstanding you, consider your last attempt to return clothing or another item to a department store.

YOUR TURN

Describe a time when a person's nonverbal messages struck you more powerfully than the words the person said.

_____

_____

_____

_____

_____

_____

_____

Was it the clerk's words, "OK, we'll exchange it," or the clerk's sigh, glare, or look of annoyance that left the stronger impression with you? Perhaps you share with your group members a tendency to believe what people show and do over what they say.

INSIGHT 20

When nonverbal messages conflict with verbal messages, we tend to believe the nonverbal messages.

Nonverbal Messages for Leaders

Conversations between leaders and team members are an ideal laboratory in which to observe (and perfect) the art of nonverbal communication. Both leaders and team members spend most of their day "communicating" (by which many people mean saying words) to all kinds of people. But the message received is often not the message intended. More important, the message received is often not acted upon.

"I think there was a time early in my career," says one company leader, "when I focused almost exclusively on saying the right words to my team members, sometimes as quickly as I could. I would even write down the approximate words I wanted to say and practice them before a team meeting. I was a living encyclopedia of how to do things, and I impressed myself with my cogent summaries of what others should be doing better. But when many of my team members came back at our next meeting with exactly the same problems and questions, I began to realize that I was pitching but they weren't catching. That's when I started taking nonverbal behavior seriously. I slowed down to make sure I had eye contact with each team member.

YOUR TURN

Describe ways in which you use nonverbal messages in your present school life or work life to get your point across and influence others.

_____

_____

_____

_____

_____

_____

_____

I watched for signs of confusion or objection. I checked often for comprehension, using such phrases as "So tell me your ideas on how we can make this happen" and "What obstacles do you see in getting this done by next week?"

This leader now has many fans among his team members. His people give him extraordinarily high marks for "really caring," "understanding me," "not talking down to me," and "helping me grasp my situation." Although members are usually not conscious of the impact of their leader's nonverbal skill, they nevertheless are influenced by these communication techniques.

INSIGHT 21

Leaders adept at using nonverbal messages are seen as particularly sensitive, caring, and approachable by team members.

Sometimes the art of nonverbal communication for leaders involves literally getting down or up to the team member's level. "When I talk to a team member, I do everything I can to get our heads at the same level. If the member is sitting in a chair, this might mean that I too pull up a chair so that we can talk eye to eye. If we're walking as we talk, I make sure that I face the person, not in a hostile way, when I want to really get a point across. Saying something as we stroll along doesn't have much impact if we're both looking ahead as we talk. The important thing is that I signal by my position, posture, and facial expressions that the person has my full attention, that I am not giving priority to my pager or phone, and that I am ready to listen for as long as it takes to hear his or her story or point of view."

The Roots of Nonverbal Communication for Leaders

Socrates' famous dictum "Know the wise man by the way he lives" was in part a warning not to trust words alone in interpreting messages from others. "Words are cheap," as the saying goes, while actions (including nonverbal cues of all kinds) tend to be much more revealing about our deep intent and attitude.

Why is it that "the eyes are windows to the soul" rather than our words alone? Probably because we do not manage the nonverbal cues we send in the many ways that we have learned to manipulate language to do our bidding. We often rehearse and package our words to achieve our ends with a listener. By contrast, we don't plan, practice, or review our nonverbal signals in our minds. These signals tend to be spontaneous, natural, and sincere—as opposed to words, which can often seem canned and manipulative.

Here's a case in point. The 2000 election year just passed recalls disingenuous debate over "the meaning of 'is'" (untrustworthy words), while on the nonverbal side media coaches did all they could to help then Vice President Gore appear less stiff and deaconish. "What he says is admirable," one commentator said during the election, "but I can't stand watching him say it." Similar effort was spent by speech coaches to help President George W. Bush eliminate the appearance of a sneer or inappropriate smile when he speaks. Both candidates understood that their nonverbal signals, especially as magnified by the television camera, were major influences on their appeal to the voting public.

YOUR TURN

Choose a well-known public figure and evaluate his or her use of nonverbal messaging. What does this person do particularly well or poorly?

_____

_____

_____

_____

_____

_____

Watching the Experts at Work

To observe masterful use of nonverbal cues, watch for the way successful salespeople relate to you. These inventive men and women know that they cannot look down at the carpet or up at the ceiling when speaking to you. Good reps know that their faces have one brief opportunity at the outset of any conversation to communicate friendliness, purpose, and cheerfulness. By the way they sit (rather than slouch) while waiting to see you, they convey their professionalism and attitude.

"After more than twenty years in the business, I don't think consciously about my nonverbal signals," says Rachel Bali, a highly successful import rep to several companies. "It just comes as second nature now to look and act the part of a winning representative for my company—someone who sincerely wants to serve the interests of people to whom I sell. In my own case, I have learned that being personable, upbeat, and direct with the people I meet on sales calls works much better than appearing aloof or unnecessarily formal. My relaxed manner doesn't stem from a lack of respect for my contacts—just the opposite. I know that if I show relaxed comfort in conversation, they will respond in kind."

INSIGHT 22

Skillful nonverbal messaging contributes to a leader's ability to achieve financial goals as well as relationship goals.

A Primer for Leaders on Nonverbal Communication Techniques

It would be folly to suggest (as some have) that certain physical behaviors automatically translate into specific communications. For example, crossed arms do not always or automatically signal that you are "closed" or uptight or hostile. We have all observed that same gesture in people who are listening intently to us and are deeply concerned about our welfare. Similarly, a pointed finger does not always signal accusation, and a clenched fist is not always a threatening display. That same fist can be a sign of exultation or victory.

All nonverbal signals and gestures take their meaning from the total context of the situation—a context they help create. The nonverbal gestures in the following list are favorites of many successful leaders, but each item in the list should be considered simply an option that may or may not fit your personal style of communication with your team members. To discover what fits and what fails for your team, you may want to try each of these techniques (as naturally as possible) while dealing with relatively minor issues. Once you've discovered your personal inventory of nonverbal techniques, you can use them at even the most urgent and crucial moments to achieve your purpose and the organization's business.

Nonverbal Cues

1. Hands flat, palms down, on the desk, table, or counter—may suggest "here's the bottom line; please take me very seriously."
2. Hands in front, with fingertips but not palms touching—may suggest "I'm listening carefully; I'm thinking, let's consider all our options; let's not rush to judgment."
3. Palms up, as if ready to receive a package—may suggest "tell me what's going on; I'm very interested."
4. Hand briefly on a team member's shoulder or a pat on the back (the upper back, thank you)—may suggest "you're not in this alone; I'm here for you; you're going to do fine."
5. Hands parallel, about six inches apart, fingers pointed up or toward the team member—may suggest "listen extremely carefully to what I'm saying; this is crucial for you to understand."
6. Eyebrows raised (but not to the point of shock or surprise)—may suggest "I'm alert and attentive to what you're telling me."
7. Eyebrows furled (but not to the point of a frown or disapproval)—may suggest "I'm not sure I understand; please go into more detail."
8. Hands clasped behind head, in a broad gesture of relaxation or stretching—may suggest "I'm relaxed about this and I want you to relax as well; talk to me without inhibition."
9. Leaning back in chair—may suggest "let's talk more generally or more casually."
10. Leaning forward in chair, closing distance between the speaker and the listener—may suggest "let's talk as specifically as possible; let's make sure we understand each other exactly."

YOUR TURN

Try several of the nonverbal techniques described earlier. Report here on the results you observed.

_____

_____

_____

_____

_____

_____

INSIGHT 23

Improving one's nonverbal messaging is not a matter of simply doing what comes naturally. Many powerful nonverbal techniques can be learned and practiced.

Again, each of these gestures must be in sync with both your words and the situation to support and enrich the total communication you intend. Many miscommunications arise, in fact, when a leader's face says one thing (perhaps a frown) and his or her words say another (perhaps "Looks OK to me" when reviewing a project or plan. The team member in this case leaves with mixed signals: "Well, the leader said things were OK, but he sure didn't look happy with them. I don't think he's telling me the whole truth."

The solution to such miscommunication lies in remembering that leader-to-member communication is neither a ballet (nonverbal gestures alone) nor a radio program (words alone) but is instead an opera (light, heavy, or soap, as you prefer) where words and gestures, including dress, combine to create the richest and most motivating or moving communication possible.

The dividends for such complete communication are paid all around: members understand and act on their leaders' advice; leaders save time by communicating powerfully and memorably, thereby avoiding repeated sermons to the same team members; and the organization thrives as word spreads about a leader "who really cares and listens."

YOUR TURN

Observe a leader you admire. What nonverbal skills can you point to that help to account for his or her effectiveness with other people?

_____

_____

_____

_____

_____

THE IMPORTANCE OF TRUTHFULNESS FOR LEADERS AND TEAM MEMBERS

Lying? Bite your tongue. No one uses that word in school or business, do they?

The habit of lying to bosses, team members, coworkers, and clients isn't polite to talk about. Nevertheless, it remains one of the primary enemies of productivity, effective leadership, and team spirit. Talk about it we must, if we envision a work or school environment where people say what they mean and do what they say.

Lying in organizations begins with the "harmless" excuses that just aren't true. Late to a meeting or work shift? Sorry, traffic on the freeway was backed up for

YOUR TURN

Tell about a time when you were the victim of an untruth told by a team member. How did you feel? How did you react?

_____

_____

_____

_____

_____

miles. (Strange, a coworker muses. The freeway was perfectly clear when I drove in.) Unwilling to make a last-minute business trip? Sorry, a good friend is going to have a minor operation this weekend and I need to be there. (How surprising when your boss runs into the two of you Saturday night at a restaurant.) In that case, the little lie must be extended: well, the operation was postponed because the doctor fell ill (with a kick under the table to signal your friend to play along).

INSIGHT 24
The temptation to lie to others begins with small fibs.

From Fibs to Fabrications

Is it just human nature to fib? Perhaps. But these threads of deception quickly weave together into a modus operandi by which organization liars con and manipulate their associates and clients. Team members or employees used to telling small lies have no trouble inventing medium-sized falsehoods for a client: "Well, we had a major computer failure that backed everything up. The technicians are here right now fixing a hard drive, and we should be able to finish everything up by tomorrow." Yeah, right.

Medium-sized lies are found particularly in three arenas of school and work life.

LEADING BY DECEPTION "If it were up to me, I would say 'yes.' But the big boss is dead set against your proposal. I'll keep trying, but it doesn't look good." In fact, the big boss never heard about your proposal. Your leader is lying as a convenient way to dodge your issues and questions. Because you don't have easy access to the big boss, there's no politically safe way to verify your leader's assertions. You're being led by deception.

DISTORTING THE CUSTOMER SATISFACTION PROCESS "No matter what the contract says, you just call me directly if you have any problems down the line. Here's my card with my direct extension." A few months after the transaction, the client does indeed call with a significant problem not covered by the contract. Then the lie must be extended: "There must have been some misunderstanding. We don't have authority to change contract terms through my department. Let me give you an 800 number for Customer Service. Someone there can probably help you." What tangled webs we weave.

DISGUISING PERFORMANCE FAILURE "My numbers may be down, but it isn't my fault. I didn't receive thorough training for my position" (or, if you prefer, "the boss played favorites" or "the competition cheated" or a host of other falsehoods). Dealing with the rippling consequences of these medium-sized lies consumes untold hours for leaders. Leadership, in fact, has been wryly described as "figuring out which of your people you can trust."

YOUR TURN

Describe a project, plan, event, or other circumstance that was negatively impacted by someone's lie. Why did the person lie? How was the truth eventually uncovered?

_____

_____

_____

_____

_____

_____

_____

_____

INSIGHT 25

Fibs quickly grow into larger lies as the liar experiences temporary success in deceiving others.

From Fabrications to Fantasy Fiction

A team member or worker adept in medium-sized lies soon graduates to the real whoppers. These are the elaborate, calculated deceptions and prevarications that often send school organizations to the dean or companies to court, set worker against worker, and shatter client relationships beyond repair. Whoppers usually occur in the following business arenas.

DESPERATE EFFORTS TO SURVIVE I'm about to get demoted or fired? Let's see which whopper will suffice. "I have been sexually harassed (or discriminated against or psychologically stressed) in the workplace." (Of course, these charges are often true and always deserve careful, fair scrutiny. But at times, they are also used as trump cards by players willing to attack others unfairly to save themselves.) Or, "I have a condition that requires accommodation." (Again, appeals to the terms of the Americans with Disabilities Act [ADA] always should be investigated carefully. But if ADA provisions are distorted by some manipulative employees to create whopper lies, everyone in the organization suffers, especially those ADA was intended to protect.)

EXCUSES FOR DISASTROUS DECISIONS I underestimated project costs by 20 percent? There's no profit left for the company, but we have to fulfill the contract nonetheless?

It's time for a whopper: "I based my decision on data provided to me by technical staff. No, that data is no longer available. For the sake of security, I destroyed it after I completed my work. But I now see how inaccurate it was—and heads should roll." (Not mine, of course. I was a victim of others' mistakes.)

EXPLANATIONS FOR GROSS INSUBORDINATION AND INTERPERSONAL CONFLICT My boss gave me yet another poor performance review. Only a whopper can turn the tables: "He has disliked me from day one in this company because I spoke my mind and wouldn't be a yes-man." (How can the boss disprove this bald falsehood? Many exemplary bosses have been tarred with the brush of calculated lies from underperformers. In response, leaders sometimes shy away from calling a spade a spade in organizations that don't support straight talk and frank judgments. Many leaders aren't willing to risk their careers by getting into a spitting match with unscrupulous accusers.)

YOUR TURN

Describe a situation in which someone's small deception eventually grew to larger, more damaging proportions as the person attempted to cover up the original lie.

_____

_____

_____

_____

_____

_____

INSIGHT 26

Lies have the potential to disrupt major business functions and destroy team relationships.

Building a Culture of Basic Truth

The negative, hand-slapping response to lying—"Liar, liar, pants on fire"—has little effect on halting the spread of prevarication in organizations. It's socially awkward to catch a liar in the act. Even if you dare to challenge a person's truthfulness on the spot, that challenge rarely changes behavior. Liars just get more proficient in order not to get caught.

To build a company culture based on telling and modeling the truth, management must commit to positive measures that

- support employees who dare to tell the truth, especially in difficult circumstances.
- allow the frank admission of error and failure as part of the learning curve on the way to excellence.
- demonstrate how business efficiency and relationships improve when lying isn't allowed as an option.

Training sessions and orientation, as well as learning materials for new and old team members and employees, are superb places to emphasize the organization's commitment to truthful statements and interaction at all levels. School newsletters and company publications can focus attention on the theme. The organization's mission, goals, and objectives can contain language that refers to truthful internal and external relationships.

Above all, performance appraisal standards can focus in part on professional integrity, not just technical competence. When lying has direct and expensive consequences in the organization, members and employees follow their self-interest in deciding to tell it like it is. Reflect for a moment on how your day as a leader would be less stressful and more productive if you could simply count on the truthfulness of what every team member or coworker says to you.

YOUR TURN

Tell about a time when you attempted to guide someone to be more truthful. How did you approach the situation? How did it turn out?

_____

_____

_____

_____

_____

_____

_____

INSIGHT 27

Individual truthfulness and integrity are easier to maintain when those values are supported and rewarded by the entire organization.

MEET A LEADER

Patricia R.
Leader for Career Day at a Northern California High School

"Don't give me a title," Patricia regularly tells administrators with whom she works on a volunteer basis at a large northern California high school. "I want everyone I contact to feel that they are leading the Career Day just as much as I am. As soon as I get a title, everyone will feel they are working for me—and that's certainly not the case." Patricia had the bright idea four years ago of bringing to campus more than 80 different professional men and women to present talks, put on demonstrations, and convey career tips to high school students considering their options for college and career. "Believe it or not," Patricia confesses, "the job takes hundreds of hours and involves more than a dozen other volunteers. We have to make contact with leaders in the workforce who can connect well with high school students (instead of just lecturing them); make sure we have buy-in from the high school faculty, who have to give up class time for our Career Day; and make all the other arrangements for food, decorations, arrival area for speakers, and follow-up evaluation of the Day. It's a big job, but I love doing it because I know lights are going on inside the heads of students as they see and hear about careers they may want to pursue." Patricia's leadership style is casual in the extreme. She holds meetings at her home, over coffee and pastries, rather than in a high school classroom. She asks each volunteer to choose what area they would enjoy working on, rather than passing out tasks indiscriminately. Above all, she keeps the project fun for all concerned, reminding them that the more they enjoy their work the more contagious their optimism will be for the participating high school faculty and students.

Summing Up

Leadership succeeds through people. This statement implies a concerted effort on a leader's part to build strong relationships with team members. These relationships depend not merely on verbal contacts (the words that pass between people) but on nonverbal messages as well. Trust between individuals depends in large part upon truthful relationships. Establishing a culture of truthfulness must therefore be a high priority for any leader.

6

Leadership by Defining Problems and Reaching Solutions

GOALS

- identify the pros and cons of different leadership styles
- isolate and offer solutions for several common leadership problems
- apply problem–solution insights to the day-to-day challenges of leadership

Leading other people is much like playing golf or tennis. Just when we think we're getting good at it, up pops a problem or situation that makes us humble again, sending us "back to school" in search of solutions.

YOUR TURN

Perhaps you have faced situations recently that remind you how difficult it can be to lead others. Describe such a situation.

_____

_____

_____

_____

_____

_____

INSIGHT 28

The art of leadership is a lifelong pursuit. We can always learn better ways to lead.

If you agree with this insight, the leadership boot camp in this chapter has a place at the table reserved for you. This update is aimed at any leader, whether experienced or inexperienced, who values a few minutes to think through the core skills and attitudes of leadership. Unlike other boot camps, this one requires no wall climbing or push-ups. Simply answer the following five questions.

ARE YOU A THEORY X OR A THEORY Y LEADER?

This famous distinction was created by Douglas MacGregor in *The Human Side of Enterprise.* Theory X leaders, he suggests, are those who believe approximately as follows:

- employees dislike work and do whatever they can to avoid it.
- bosses maintain control primarily by threats and punishment.
- tasks must be kept simple so that dull-witted employees can learn them and then do them over and over.[7]

We've all had at least one Theory X leader in our careers. This leader was the one who expected us to fail, emphasized the negative whenever possible, and made it seem that each day on the job might be our last. Not surprisingly, most of us did not develop much loyalty for this kind of boss. We may have cowered when he or she caught us face-to-face, but inside we were boiling. Not surprisingly, we quit that job as soon as possible for a better opportunity. (Note that it wasn't a matter of pay. The number one reason for resignations across industries is "I couldn't stand my boss.")

YOUR TURN

Tell about a Theory X leader or manager from your past or present. How would you describe your feelings about this individual?

_____

_____

_____

_____

_____

INSIGHT 29

Theory X leaders believe employees must be driven to perform.

By contrast, a Theory Y leader holds different assumptions about his or her people:

- employees generally enjoy their jobs and seek to do them well.
- bosses gain loyalty by showing respect for employees, listening to their perspectives, and looking out for their interests.
- employees are good at problem solving and want to make decisions on their own that affect the quality of their work.

Think about your own attitudes toward your employees. Probably a few come to mind who need the strict command-and-control approaches of Theory X leadership. But, in general, would you not agree that your people are well-intentioned, smart, and skilled at what they do? Even if you answer, "Well, some of them, perhaps," there's good leadership sense in treating employees under Theory Y assumptions. When you believe the best about your people and treat them as talented contributors, they tend to produce in kind. This isn't Pollyannaish leadership. It is a strategic choice to emphasize the positive, expect the best, and reward performance more often than punishing failure.

YOUR TURN

Describe a Theory Y leader you have experienced or heard about. How do your impressions of this individual differ from those you have of the Theory X leader you described earlier?

_____

_____

_____

_____

_____

_____

INSIGHT 30

Theory Y leaders believe that employees can be trusted to perform.

DO YOU PRACTICE *LEADERSHIP BY GETTING MAD?*

Leadership by getting mad (LGM) is closely allied to Theory X principles. A leader who thinks of employees as bad children easily falls into the role of angry parent. By wearing a foul mood for all to see and blustering at every opportunity, the LGM leader tries to drive employees with the stick of anger. To be fair, such anger does produce short-term results. Yell and swear at employees for showing up late for work, and they will indeed start showing up more promptly—until they don't show up at all, having found what they consider a better job and a better boss. You may be mad inside over employee tardiness, but what you feel should not automatically dictate how you act to achieve your goals.

Anger has no long-term value for motivating employees to change behavior or achieve goals. Worse, anger eventually backfires on the red-faced leader who practices it. If the leader uses a temper tantrum to get employees hopping one day, what does he or she do for an encore the following day or week? Scream louder? Rise to new levels of profanity? The Dartmouth Heart Study, involving thousands of leaders and others, pointed to anger as a prime contributor to fatal or career-interrupting heart problems and other health consequences. The stick of anger ends up stabbing those who wield it. (This is not to say that good leaders don't ever show anger. They do, often with justification. But good leaders don't make anger the primary means by which they motivate employees to do their jobs. They don't put on their game face of anger as a daily habit when entering the office.)

YOUR TURN

Describe a time when you were managed by anger. How did you react?

_____

_____

_____

_____

_____

_____

INSIGHT 31

A leader's anger has only short-term power in motivating performance.

DO YOU WALK THE TALK?

Socrates' idea "Know the wise man by the way he lives" is applicable here, as earlier. Today, words are cheaper than ever when it comes to leadership effectiveness. Employees quickly start hearing only "yada, yada, yada" when a leader harps on procedures and work habits that he or she does not practice himself or herself. For example, it's hard to give courteous customer service when you work for a boss who can't or won't give courteous employee service. Gandhi could have been speaking directly to modern leaders when he said, "Become the change that you seek in the world." Telling others what you want them to do easily gets lost in the shadow of what you yourself do as a leader.

The message here is easier to agree with than to practice, as the Marine Corps discovered during the last devastating floods in the Mississippi River states. Marines and other military personnel were brought in to do the backbreaking work of filling and moving sandbags to keep floodwaters away from homes and businesses. Having a sergeant yell commands from a distance was not nearly as effective—in terms of sandbags filled—as having the sergeant get knee-deep in the muck and do his or her part in the toughest parts of the job. It's almost impossible not to follow your boss's lead when he or she is working hard in the trenches beside you.

This is not to say that leaders should micromanage every aspect of the work they supervise. But employees should see the leader as someone who is willing to pitch in to accomplish the goal at hand—someone for whom all kinds of work are respected and worth doing. Many Fortune 500 CEOs make it a regular part of their job to get "out on the line"—not as a way of showing regular employees how to do things better but instead to show interest and involvement in the nitty-gritty of the business. Employees consider such bosses "one of us" and redouble their efforts for them.

YOUR TURN

Recall a time when a leader pitched in with the most difficult tasks facing a team. How did the team react?

_____

_____

_____

_____

_____

_____

INSIGHT 32

What a leader does underlines and gives credibility to what a leader says.

DO YOU PLAY FAIR WITH YOUR PEOPLE?

Employees look beyond their paychecks in deciding whether they are content and motivated at their jobs. They consider equity and fairness in determining how hard to work, whether to go the extra mile, or whether to quit. As discussed more thoroughly in Chapter 7, here is the essential equity proposition:

$$\frac{\text{My reward}}{\text{My input}} \text{ should equal } \frac{\text{Your reward}}{\text{Your input}}$$

No employee grouses when someone who gives a lot in the company also gets a lot in terms of salary and respect. But morale can slip away quickly when company rewards seem to be out of whack with employee effort. It's the rare employee who can press on to do the job right when others around him or her are kicking back but receiving the same pay.

Good leaders keep the equity equation constantly in mind as they assign jobs, promote employees, pay out bonuses or perks, and do performance evaluations. Like skilled referees, they want everyone on the field to know that the game is guided by rules, not by whim, chance, or favoritism.

YOUR TURN

Describe a time when you felt that you were doing more than your fair share of work on a team. How did you react? How did things turn out?

_____

_____

_____

_____

_____

INSIGHT 33

Team members do not willingly sustain long periods of perceived unfairness in workload versus reward. Performance will fall off dramatically if the perceived unfairness is not corrected.

ARE YOU AN EGO-LEADER OR A SERVANT-LEADER?

Because leaders typically make more money and have more job security than the rest of the crew, these leaders may be tempted to spell "me" with a capital "M." We have all met and perhaps worked for leaders who rarely seek advice because they know it all—leaders who seldom listen because they are so busy talking. In effect, they play the "mind" of the work group and let everyone else play the role of body parts. The failure of this anatomy lies in a natural tendency for unused organs to atrophy. Employees quickly get the idea that it's OK to park their own brains at the door when they enter work because the boss doesn't expect them to think on the job.

YOUR TURN

Describe a leader you believe to be driven largely by ego needs. Then describe a second leader who appears to serve out of a commitment to the needs of others.

_____

_____

_____

_____

INSIGHT 34

Leadership proves ineffective when team members believe that the leader values only his or her own opinion and perspective.

MEET A LEADER

Tom E.
Organizing Student Tour Guide for College Orientation

"Before I came aboard," Tom says, "campus tours were carried out by four older employees of the university. The so-called tours were made up of a quick ride around campus in a golf cart. Every evaluation of new student orientation showed that the campus tours were the lowest rated aspect of their first days on campus. I volunteered, therefore, to give what I called "the student perspective tour" to parents and new student arrivals. Instead of using a golf cart and hurrying them through a 20-minute drive around campus, my friends and I (acting as tour guides for separate groups) took them on a leisurely stroll, stopping often to tell them not just the bare facts about the university but also to communicate some of the history, lore, and even gossip that had accumulated over the years. Students and their parents always had the opportunity to ask questions or make comments at any time on our tours. Within a matter of months, the campus tour conducted "our way" rose to the top of the ratings scale on new student orientation. The university hired me on a part-time basis to oversee and enhance this personal approach to campus touring. As a result, we are seeing an 18 percent increase in students who decide to enroll in our university instead of elsewhere. The opportunity to play a creative leadership role in solving a major problem for the university gives me great satisfaction. When I graduate, I think my ability to analyze a problem and come up with affordable, innovative solutions will serve me well no matter what industry sector I eventually join as an employee. The whole experience also spurred my motivation to seek out leadership roles. It has been a lot of work but also a lot of fun to see my plan become reality, for the good of new students and the university."

Summing Up

Good leaders empower their people to meet challenges, solve problems, and invent better ways of doing the job. When the work team is fully committed to this path, the leader at times becomes almost invisible. Each employee focuses so intently on doing the job right that no taskmaster or big cheese comes into the picture. In this scenario, the leader can truly become what most heads of organizations would prefer to be—mentors, coaches, and cheerleaders for those out on the field for the organization.

7

Leadership by Motivating

GOALS

- recognize powerful motivators beyond financial rewards
- use these motivators to build strong work teams
- practice leadership strategies based on motivation techniques

It's payday. In a ritual dating back to ancient China, you hand an employee a piece of paper representing wages earned and benefits provided. Nods are exchanged but seldom any words. Or, the check may simply go into the mail or direct deposit without any communication at all. Many leaders view the paycheck as the prime stimulus—perhaps the only stimulus—to employee productivity and retention. Usually, such leaders get what they pay for: no more, no less.

THE SHRINKING POWER OF MONEY AS A MOTIVATOR

This chapter explores professional life for leaders and managers beyond the paycheck. What makes a top performer in your company or industry? What keeps your best hands from jumping ship? What makes workers want to give their best effort to procedures and projects?

Not the paycheck alone. In fact, "throwing money at the problem" to improve performance has proven notoriously ineffective in everything from union negotiations to U. S. foreign policy. Consider two realities of work life:

- Almost all workers need more money than they receive. These needs are far from frivolous. Leaders and managers are trying to save for their children's college expenses and their own retirement. Workers in the "sandwich generation" find themselves financially responsible both for their own children and for their aging parents. Single parents face child-care expenses that may effectively reduce their take-home salaries to minimum wage.

• No leader or owner can afford to pay employees what they need. Take-home pay may meet the bills but never the needs and wants.

Fortunately, workers show up each morning for *more* than the paycheck. Leaders who know why this is so are legends in their companies—those rare individuals who spend time and attention on their employees in addition to providing wages.

YOUR TURN

Describe a previous or current job in which money was not the prime motivator for your performance. What other factors influenced you to do your best?

_____

_____

_____

_____

_____

_____

_____

INSIGHT 35

Money alone does not explain on-the-job motivation.

THE INVOLVEMENT FACTOR

Newcomers to companies may typically be more driven by money because they have built few social bonds at the company, have little ego involvement with long-term projects or planning, and have slight personal identification with the fate of the company.

But as the months of employment turn into years, the involvement factor begins to grow as a motivator. Old-timers do work in part for the pay, of course, but there are also at play the many coworker relations, interesting tasks, respect from superiors and subordinates, and that "settled-in" feeling for the workplace as a surrogate home. (To make this point in an extreme way, consider the owners, leaders, and managers who have made their fortunes and could retire in luxury but still continue to show up at the office every day.)

It is no exaggeration to say that the primary challenge of every leader is to understand and use the involvement factor as a management tool for growing the company and achieving its mission. What is offered here is a "mini-MBA" on the components of the involvement factor—what it is, how to use it, and with whom.

YOUR TURN

Recall a job in which your motivation grew over time. What factors accounted for this increase in motivation?

_____

_____

_____

_____

_____

_____

_____

_____

INSIGHT 36

As team members become more involved with one another and with team projects, their motivation to perform increases.

The Light Goes On

The importance of the involvement factor was first recognized in 1924 in the surprising results of a somewhat bizarre experiment conducted by efficiency experts at the Western Electric Company at its Hawthorne, Illinois, plant. Following usual scientific methods, researchers selected a test group of employees and a comparable control group to gauge the effects of various levels of lighting on worker productivity. Lighting in the room occupied by the test group was gradually increased. As expected, the productivity of the test group rose as illumination increased.

But to the surprise of the researchers, the productivity of the control group also rose without any change in their illumination. Lighting was reduced at one point to the level of moonlight for the test group, and productivity increased again. Researchers found that the only way they could cause productivity to dip for either group was to darken the rooms so that employees literally could not see.

These unusual results attracted the interest of Harvard's Elton Mayo. During a two-year period, Mayo and his team tried all manner of workplace enhancements upon test groups—longer rest breaks, company-paid lunches, more comfortable workstations, and so forth. To their astonishment, control groups without any of these enhancements performed as well as or better than the test groups.

Finally, researchers took away all work enhancements from the test groups and plunged them back to their original work conditions. Surely, researchers thought, we will now see productivity plummet as workers react negatively to these changes. Just the opposite occurred. Productivity for the test groups reached an all-time high.

What had happened here? As John Schemerhorn writes in *Managing Organizational Behavior,* "Two factors were singled out as having special importance in this regard. First, there was a positive group development in the test room. The operators shared both good social relations with one another and a common desire to do a good job. Second, supervision was more participative than that otherwise experienced by the operators. Operators in the test room were made to feel important, given a lot of information and frequently consulted for their opinion on what was taking place."[8]

In short, workers felt involved and performed accordingly. Ever since, the exceptional performance of any group singled out for special attention has been labeled the "Hawthorne effect." These results gave rise to the human relations movement (and HR departments or responsibilities in virtually every company). Following the Hawthorne studies, the word was out that workplace motivation involved much more than payroll dollars.

YOUR TURN

Tell about a time when you and your team (or you alone) were in the spotlight in some way. What effect did this attention have on your performance?

_____

_____

_____

_____

_____

INSIGHT 37

Team members generally enjoy special attention and do their best work under such circumstances.

Four Components of the Involvement Factor

Asking just how the involvement factor works in school and business environments is an invitation to a quick tour of the four "big discoveries" in employee motivation in the last hundred years. Each of these components can provide workers with an extra incentive beyond the paycheck—with healthy results for the company.

THE NEEDS COMPONENT   What do your employees *need* from their jobs? Psychologist David McClelland and his coworkers approached this question by asking workers to view pictures and then write brief stories about them. Three executives, for example, were individually given a photograph that shows a man sitting down and looking at family photos arranged on his work desk. When asked to write about the picture, one executive wrote about a manager who was daydreaming about a family picnic the next day. The second executive described a product designer who had his family to thank for his latest bright idea. The third executive saw a structural manager confidently at work on a bridge-stress problem.

From the evidence provided by thousands of such test samples, McClelland put forth the three needs most commonly expressed by workers:

- *Need for achievement.* Workers with a high need for achievement want individual responsibility, frequent feedback, and challenging goals.
- *Need for affiliation.* Workers with a high need for affiliation want fulfilling interpersonal relationships at work and opportunities to communicate often with coworkers and clients.
- *Need for power.* Workers with a high need for power want to exercise influence over others and gain attention and recognition for their status.

As you consider your school or workplace, you probably don't need to administer paper-and-pencil tests to determine which group members or employees are prone to particular needs. Leaders who know their employees usually have a quite accurate idea of what each person needs.

The key, then, to motivation through needs is obvious: *give employees what they need.* For example, you can manage a worker with a high need for affiliation by giving him or her liaison, coordinator, or other interpersonal responsibility. The task force or committee assignment that may sound burdensome and repulsive to you will probably sound attractive and motivating to the employee with affiliation needs.

Manage the worker with a high need for power by assigning supervisory responsibility—and expecting results. Manage the worker with a high need for achievement by using the manage-by-objectives approach. Set forth clear, challenging goals with associated feedback points and rewards for performance.

This needs-based approach to motivation worked well for Fran Varner, vice president of marketing at Fillauer, Inc., in Chattanooga, Tennessee. Her needs were met as she rose from an entry-level position to the VP level. "Fillauer has encouraged and challenged me through my 16 years by providing various types of education and training," Varner says. "I am proud to be associated with my company because they invest in people, not just machinery and computers, and they reap the reward from their investment through many long-term and committed employees."

When leaders understand what needs an individual employee has and uses those needs to identify salient rewards, then involvement and motivation will naturally follow.

YOUR TURN

Choose three members on a work team you know well. Specify what you believe to be the primary needs of each individual from the team experience.

_____

_____

_____

_____

_____

_____

INSIGHT 38

Leaders who know what individual workers need can motivate these people by fulfilling those needs.

THE EXPECTANCY COMPONENT A second aspect of the involvement factor stems from the work of Victor Vroom. He described motivation as a "yes" answer to three questions:

- Are you able to perform or accomplish the task?
- Does your performance bring you a predictable result?
- Do you value that result?

If a worker answers "yes" to all three questions, then he or she will be motivated to expend maximum or near-maximum effort on work tasks. But even one "no" answer breaks the chain and minimizes motivation.

For example, a worker might answer "no" to the second question, feeling that strong performance is recognized only haphazardly in the company. This worker would not be highly motivated—the results of his or her effort are too unpredictable.

Obviously, a leader's goal in a manufacturing environment should be to ensure that workers can answer "yes" to all three elements of Vroom's motivation formula. A leader can affect how each question is answered by providing support and resources so a worker is able to perform, being clear about what rewards employees will receive, and knowing what rewards employees value. In particular, leaders must make sure that *performance predictably leads to results that workers value.*

YOUR TURN

Describe some aspect of your life in which you are motivated more by expectancy than by other forms of rewards.

_____

_____

_____

_____

_____

_____

INSIGHT 39

What people expect to happen in the future is a powerful motivator for their actions in the present.

THE EQUITY COMPONENT A third component of the involvement factor has to do with perceived fairness. Inevitably, workers in a manufacturing environment compare what they do and receive with what others do and receive in the company. If they feel an inequity as a result of that comparison, that perception can become a powerful factor in determining motivational levels. Few other traditional motivators—including salary, reputation, or challenging work—can overcome the deep burn felt by a worker who feels cheated.

J. Stacy Adams is the father of equity theories of motivation. His equation for equity is straightforward:

$$\frac{\text{My reward}}{\text{My input}} \text{ should equal } \frac{\text{Your reward}}{\text{Your input}}$$

When the sides of the equation balance, we're satisfied and proceed with work in a motivated way. But when the balance tilts heavily against us, we often act out our frustration and sense of injustice. This acting out may mean "paying back" those in the company who established the inequitable situation. Or, a worker may reduce input (in the form of less effort or involvement) to balance the equity equation again. Finally, a worker may criticize other employees for what they do or receive, again in an effort to balance the equity equation.

Leaders can prevent equity warfare in a company by distributing work responsibilities and related rewards as fairly as possible. Clear differences among employees can be established by distinguishing job titles, job descriptions, chains of reporting, numbers of employees supervised, and types of rewards distributed. In this way, workers have fewer direct points of comparison when evaluating the fairness of their own situations.

YOUR TURN

Tell about a time when you or someone you know pointed out an unfair work situation to a manager. How was the situation resolved?

_____

_____

_____

_____

_____

_____

INSIGHT 40

A team member tends to measure his or her workload and rewards against those of other team members, not against some absolute standard.

THE ATTITUDE COMPONENT The final component in the involvement factor focuses broadly on worker attitudes in relation to motivation. Frederick Herzberg asked more than 4,000 workers to respond to two statements:

- "Tell me about a time when you felt exceptionally good about your job."
- "Tell me about a time when you felt exceptionally bad about your job."

While analyzing the responses to these statements, Herzberg and his team saw a clear pattern emerge. When people wanted to express satisfaction with their jobs, they named a predictable list of things they liked. Herzberg called these items "satisfiers" or "motivators." But when it came to dissatisfaction with their jobs, people did not list the absence of satisfiers, as might be expected. Instead, they came up with a separate list of items Herzberg called "dissatisfiers."

Here, first, are the top six satisfiers identified by Herzberg:

- achievement
- recognition
- the work itself

- responsibility
- advancement
- growth

By contrast, here are the top six dissatisfiers from his study:

- company policy and administration
- supervision
- relationship with supervisor
- work conditions
- relationships with peers
- relationships with subordinates

To avoid employee dissatisfaction (and its accompanying lack of motivation), a leader must take care of the dissatisfiers (that is, with fair supervision, adequate work conditions, and so forth). But to go to the next step and *truly motivate* an employee, a leader must develop a reward system that focuses on the satisfiers. Keep in mind that what is necessary (preventing dissatisfaction) is not sufficient to motivate. A leader's top priority should be to promote satisfiers rather than to remove dissatisfiers. Taking away problems in the form of dissatisfiers does not produce a motivated employee. Only the presence of satisfiers can do that.

YOUR TURN

Call to mind a leadership role you once played or now play. In what ways were or are you involved in removing dissatisfiers for your team members? In what ways were or are you involved in providing satisfiers for these individuals?

_____

_____

_____

_____

_____

_____

INSIGHT 41

Removing what is wrong with a job does not by itself make the job satisfying. Leaders must take the additional step of promoting satisfying aspects of the work as perceived by team members.

Finding the Right Fit

Needs, expectancy, equity, attitude—which motivational component of the involvement factor best fits your workforce? Leaders can answer this question only by getting to know their employees well. Paul Hersey and Kenneth Blanchard warn leaders not to assume that their own motivators are identical with their workers' motivators. As Hersey and Blanchard's studies have shown, what's high on a leader's list of motivators may be low on a worker's (see Table 7.1).

Notice in particular that "good wages" ranks number 1 for supervisors but only number 5 for workers. Because a 10 percent raise might send a leader over the moon with joy, one might assume that a 10 percent raise would be similarly motivating for an entry-level employee. But remembering that "good wages" rated no more than a 5 for workers, it may turn out that entry-level workers raised from $6.10 to $6.71 (a 10 percent raise) may not be motivated to work like John Henry. Many Generation X employees, in fact, may yawn.

TABLE 7.1 Priority of wanted job aspects

(1 = highest)	Supervisor's Rank	Worker's Rank
Good working conditions	4	9
Feeling "in" on things	10	2
Tactful discipline	7	10
Appreciation for work done	8	1
Management loyalty to workers	6	8
Good wages	1	5
Promotion and growth with company	3	7
Understanding of personal problems	9	3
Job security	2	4
Interesting work	5	6

Source: Paul Hersey and Kenneth Blanchard, as cited in *Motivating People,* by Dayle Smith (1997).

YOUR TURN

Create your own score sheet of Wanted Job Aspects, using the categories in Table 7.1. Compare your entries with those of your classmates or team members. How do you explain the differences?

_____

_____

_____

_____

_____

INSIGHT 42

Team members of different ages, positions of responsibility, and salary ranges will identify quite different priorities in what they want from a job.

COMMITTING TO THE INVOLVEMENT FACTOR

Especially in economic times when increasing shareholder value may mean freezing pay levels for workers, the involvement factor becomes a crucial set of tools for leaders seeking to boost morale and productivity. Payday can be only a part of the effective leader's panoply of motivational strategies—and often not the most important part.

MEET A LEADER

Ruiz J.
Green Coordinator for a Small Corporation

"When I came to my present job as accounting supervisor," Ruiz relates, "I couldn't help but notice that the company was wasting a lot of its resources, and expensively so. Lights, computers, and other energy-consumers were left on all night. Information that could have been quickly and accurately shared by electronic means was sent around in hard copy, costing the company thousands of dollars in unnecessary paper costs. Most of these paper copies were almost immediately discarded by employees, leading to a further ecological problem. Even though I was a relatively new employee, I decided to step forward to let management know about their wasteful practices and to suggest some easy fixes. At our first meeting, my bosses were noticeably suspicious about my motives and plans. They wondered how much all these ideas were going to cost the company and how my plans would add more work to their jobs. I began by showing them the bottom-line cost savings of better energy practices and less wasteful use of paper, print cartridges, and other office supplies. Without exaggerating in the least, I was able to show them that the company could save more than $100,000 per quarter simply by getting people to turn off unnecessary lights, shut down stand-by electronic equipment such as printers and computers, and invest in energy-efficient heating and illumination practices. Within six months, these measures were being practiced throughout the company. The savings turned out to be more than even I had anticipated. To my delight, the CEO of the company created a special position (paid for in part by the energy savings) called director of environmental practices and offered me the job. I jumped at it, since it was an area where my passion and expertise joined. I will admit that I took a bit of a risk at first in sticking my neck out as a leader. But in my case it certainly paid off, for my own career, for company profits, and for the environment."

Summing Up

Motivating by the Needs Component

- An employee's individual needs can be discerned by a leader through listening and observing.
- Leaders' own needs are not a template for determining employees' needs.

Motivating by the Expectancy Component

- Employees will devote more effort to achieving goals that they think are attainable.
- Leaders must help affect how employees view their ability to do the job.
- For maximum motivation, employees must value the rewards they expect to receive.

Motivating by the Equity Component

- Leaders must know what job titles, duties, and salaries employees are likely to use for comparison with their situations.

- Leaders must structure work organizations to prevent unproductive comparisons by workers.
- Leaders can control information about jobs and salaries to influence comparisons.

Motivating by the Attitude Component

- Eliminating poor working conditions does not automatically create a motivating work climate.
- Leaders should give priority to providing satisfiers (motivators) and preventing dissatisfiers.

8

Leadership by Delegating Tasks and Responsibilities

GOALS

- recognize the limitations of the "lone wolf" leader
- grasp four aspects of leadership that can be shared advantageously
- practice delegation in a way that strengthens the abilities and motivation of group members

No leader "does it alone"—at least for long. We all depend on others for their ideas, help, and encouragement. This chapter focuses on productive ways not only to distribute work responsibilities to the members of a work team but also to motivate them to accomplish those tasks.

"LONE WOLF" LEADERS

Too many student leaders and business leaders think of themselves as lone wolves. And no wonder: our ideas of leadership have certainly been shaped more by the movies than by the dictionary. We have all watched Hollywood stars portray leaders as unique, almost superhuman beings who stand apart from the crowd. These loners "do it their way"—Russell Crowe in *Gladiator,* Julia Roberts in *Erin Brockovich,* Harrison Ford in *Air Force One,* and virtually all of the roles of such actors as Clint Eastwood, Bruce Willis, Sean Connery, and their clan. It would not be hard to conclude that a leader knows more, does more, risks more, and reaps more than the average person. Above all, a leader is portrayed as someone who does not depend on others.

That's a heavy load to carry to the campus or the workplace each day for men and women who lead their organizations in some role. It's just plain exhausting to be a leader in the Hollywood sense—a go-it-alone, my-way-or-the-highway individual who believes the organization would fold immediately were it not for his or her 18-hour days.

YOUR TURN

We have all met at least one "lone wolf" leader. Choose an individual from your experience who attempts to lead without much assistance from others. What are the pros and cons of his or her leadership style?

_____

_____

_____

_____

_____

_____

INSIGHT 43

Actual leaders are less the individual hero portrayed by movies and more the skilled facilitator valued by team members.

SHARED LEADERSHIP

Fortunately, there is another less publicized but more practical way to be an influential, effective leader in the university or business world. The shared approach to leadership may not win Oscars, but it definitely promotes good management of organizations large and small.

Specifically, you as a leader can share four aspects of leadership with key people in the organization: vision, relationship, decision making, and tasks.

Share the Vision

Legend has it that a young man stopped on a dusty French path in the late Middle Ages to watch a laborer chipping away pieces from a large stone. "What are you doing?" he asked the worker. "I'm trying to make this round stone square," came the sullen reply. The young man walked a bit farther and saw another laborer hammering away at a similar block of stone. "What are you doing?" he asked. The worker replied, "I'm doing my job. I'm a stonemason." Farther still down the path, the young man encountered a third laborer who was also working a heavy piece of stone. "What are you doing?" the young man asked. The worker looked up and replied, "I'm building a cathedral."

This is vision—the ability to see what can be if you work smart and hard. No leader should keep such vision to himself or herself. In meetings, memos, and ordinary work conversation, the leader should welcome others into the vision. The others' commitment to the organization and loyalty to the leader will increase dramatically as they begin to see the larger picture—the reasons behind leadership decisions, the goals for college or company programs, and the long-term potential for the organization and its members.

YOUR TURN

Describe a leader (perhaps one of your bosses or college associates) who is adept at sharing the vision. How does such sharing affect your relationships to the leader and the organization?

_____

_____

_____

_____

_____

_____

INSIGHT 44

When a leader shares his or her vision, he or she enables team members to work toward that vision and make it their own.

Share Relationships

Lee Iacocca said it well: "In the end, all business operations can be reduced to three words: people, product, and profits. But people come first. Unless you've got a good team, you can't do much with the other two."[9] A leader not only has good working relationships with his or her peers or employees but also urges those people to *share relationships with one another.* In short, the leader builds a work team.

As in basketball, baseball, hockey, and football, the team—rather than any individual player—wins the game. In a college or business context, a healthy work team exhibits five characteristics:

1. The team places high value on sharing information and on being responsible as a group for problem solving. The leader asks questions more often than he or she gives orders.
2. The team downplays power relations (the "pecking order") within its structure and instead emphasizes the relative equality of each team member. The leader doesn't wear a crown to work.
3. The team encourages and rewards team spirit and cooperation in meeting or exceeding expectations. The atmosphere for a team should be that of the Ryder Cup—all members pulling for one another—rather than that of a tournament with just one winner.
4. Team members handle conflict within the team by themselves whenever possible. The leader doesn't make a regular practice of calling people on the carpet. (It wears out both the leader and the carpet.)
5. Team members share team successes equally. The leader doesn't take all the credit.

YOUR TURN

Choose some past or present leadership experience of your own, large or small. In what ways do you feel you could have improved in the category of sharing relationships?

_____

_____

_____

_____

_____

_____

INSIGHT 45

When team relationships have high priority, team members perform in an atmosphere of mutual trust rather than under the threat of being dropped from the team.

Share Decision Making

Some leaders make the mistake of surrounding themselves with subordinates who can be counted on to agree with the leader's position no matter what. Social psychologist Irving Janis studied this tendency and called it "groupthink." Some subordinates may go along with the boss's ideas out of a misguided sense of loyalty. Others may be yes-people because they fear the boss's anger.

Is groupthink ruining the decision-making power of your team? Yes, if your people believe any of the following.

- "No one working in this organization should buck the opinions of the leader."
- "Information that doesn't agree with the leader's position must be incorrect."
- "Only one position can be right."
- "If a group member has private reservations about a decision, policy, or plan, it's best not to mention it."
- "There's little need to discuss work topics thoroughly, since the leader has probably already done so."

I. L. Janis points to the Bay of Pigs fiasco as the consummate example of group-think: "The group that deliberated on the Bay of Pigs decision included people of considerable talent. Like the President, all of the main advisors were shrewd thinkers, capable of objective rational analysis, and accustomed to speaking their minds. But collectively they failed to detect the serious flaws in the invasion plan."[10]

Does the history of your organization involve one or more miniature Bay of Pigs misadventures? Can you call to mind plans or projects that went terribly wrong? If so, consider the decision making that led to such problems. In many cases, you may find that the pitfalls could have been avoided if only the right people had spoken up—and had been empowered to speak up—as part of the usual decision-making process in the organization.

YOUR TURN

Choose an organization with which you are familiar. Describe how important decisions are made within that organization. Should decision making be shared more completely with group members? If so, how?

_____

_____

_____

_____

_____

_____

The clear alternative to groupthink at your college organization or company is a decision-making environment in which every contributor feels obligated to give his or her best judgment, no matter if it conflicts with the party line or opinions of the leader. A leader can encourage this kind of decision-making network by (a) seeking out and listening attentively to other points of view; (b) praising or otherwise rewarding all whose insights contributed to the decision, including those critical of the decision itself; and (c) educating key people in the organization on the importance of diversity of opinion and independence of mind.

INSIGHT 46

Groupthink reflects a lack of confidence by team members in expressing their individual opinions, perhaps out of fear of alienation or ridicule by the group or the group leader.

Share Tasks Through Delegation

In the early decades of the twentieth century, leadership researcher Napoleon Hill conducted in-depth interviews with many successful leaders, including Theodore Roosevelt, Henry Ford, Thomas Edison, George Eastman, John D. Rockefeller, Clarence Darrow, and scores of other notables. Hill concluded that not one of these leaders was truly self-made. All had relied on the talents and goodwill of those who worked with them and for them. The inscription on the tombstone of steel magnate Andrew Carnegie captured the truth: "Here lies one who knew how to get around him men who were cleverer than himself."

Shrewd leaders learn early in their careers to maximize their influence on any given project by welcoming the participation of talented subordinates. The art of leadership, in fact, has coyly been described as the process of turning one's work over to others.

Some leaders fear delegation because "others won't do it right," "I'll lose control," or "I'll lose face." These are the leaders who take on too much work and end up hating the career they thought they wanted. Although delegation depends on the personalities and situations or circumstances at your organization, the following guidelines may put you on the path to strategic delegation.

- Delegate tasks in such a way that they fit in with the subordinate's development. Delegation, after all, is a powerful training function. Rather than distributing tasks randomly, determine in advance which tasks make the best sense for a particular member's or employee's growth with the organization.
- Mix hard and easy, long and quick tasks in delegating to subordinates. In some organizations, employees associate delegation with drudgery, largely because the leader off-loads onto them only the most unpleasant, time-consuming tasks. Wise leaders keep track of which members or employees have gotten the short end of the delegation stick lately.
- Be specific about responsibilities, reporting requirements, and performance measures. Too many leaders assume that group members or subordinates can read their minds about such expectations. Be clear in telling your key people what you wish them to accomplish, how and when they should report progress or problems, and how you will determine how well the job is being done.
- Support the group member or subordinate with the same or greater resources that you would provide for yourself in accomplishing the task. Consider in advance what information, contacts, support personnel, equipment, funding, and other support the subordinate will require in fulfilling the delegated responsibility.

LEADERSHIP FOR SMALLER GROUPS

Just as America is a country dominated by small businesses, so leadership occurs much more often with smaller groups rather than large populations. Leading a small group—your work unit of five people at the job, for example—makes use of the same principles taught here for motivating, guiding, and listening to thousands. In fact, leading a small group often proves more challenging than leading a large group for three reasons:

1. The small group gets to know the leader. In a small-group environment, the leader's sincerity and deep intentions can't be "spun" by clever handlers, as is sometimes the case in national political leadership races. Members of the small group see their leader every day and sometimes even every hour. They not only take the measure of the man or woman who is their leader, but take it dozens of times each week. The leader of a small group can't hide out.

2. The small group has access to its leader to ask questions, voice concerns, and register protests. On the large scale of national politics, the president may go for months at a time without allowing a public press conference. Not so with the small group leader. Passing another worker in the hall becomes an occasion for a question; pausing for coffee opens up a conversation about what the leader thinks. Leaders of small groups can't "stonewall" their followers. Concerns have to be answered often and honestly.

3. The small group usually has the strong expectation of consensus decision making and will criticize a leader who is unwilling to work toward such consensus. When hundreds of thousands of followers are involved, the leader inevitably faces the reality that a portion of the group—perhaps a significant portion—simply doesn't agree with his or her position. The leader nevertheless goes ahead and makes a decision in spite of the lack of consensus. Not so in a small group environment. If in a group of five people three agree with the group leader and two disagree, the leader would be ill-advised to blithely "call a vote" and proceed on the basis of a 3 to 2 majority. That kind of rigid decision making on the part of the leader would no doubt result in productivity paralysis for the small group. More likely, the leader would discuss the issue at hand with the group until all members had indicated at least a willingness to go along with one plan of action, even if one or two

---

YOUR TURN

Describe a time that you delegated a task or responsibility to someone else. How did it turn out? What aspects of such delegation do you feel are most important for success?

_____

_____

_____

_____

_____

members were less than enthused about that prospect. The leader of a small group can't afford dissension in the same way that the leader of a large group can.

INSIGHT 47

Delegation involves both the leader's trust that a team member can accomplish an assigned duty and the leader's support for the team member's efforts.

Management guru Peter Drucker captured the nature and wisdom of distributed leadership well: "The leader of the past was a person who knew how to tell. The leader of the future will be a person who knows how to ask."[11]

DELEGATION TO THE APATHETIC OR UNWILLING

Finally, we must qualify our enthusiasm for the involvement factor by admitting that leaders often face the dilemma of having to assign work to those who, frankly, don't want to do it. When all the motivators discussed in this section have been tried without success, a leader is left with the option to exercise blunt organizational power: "Jack, you signed on to do a particular job in this company. The work I am assigning you is directly in line with those job responsibilities. You're welcome to come to me with any problems you're experiencing along the way, but I do expect you to complete this job assignment by the date specified."

The source of an employee's apathy or unwillingness to give his or her best effort may be difficult to discover. No organizational leader should take this negative attitude personally ("Jack just doesn't like working for me"). It is usually more accurate, and certainly more constructive, to make the assumption that Jack is facing problems in his personal life that are influencing his professional productivity. If these problems can be discussed, perhaps one of the many programs in the company's Employee Assistance Program (EAP) can be helpful in resolving the matter. But the workplace should never be a psychiatrist's couch for each and every problem experienced by employees. Workers in most organizations understand that employment termination is a real possibility if delegated work is continually ignored or done poorly.

MEET A LEADER

Jennifer P.
Western Regional Sales Manager for a Major Clothing Chain.

"I faced a head-on moral dilemma beginning with my first day on the job," says Jennifer P. "We have 120 stores, located primarily in malls and catering to middle-to-low-income clothes shoppers—which, in this economy, turns out to be millions of people! My boss sat me down and said, 'Jennifer, you have to understand one thing about our company. We don't care so much if they buy our clothes. More than anything else we want to be the ones who get a Visa or Mastercard in their hands. These shoppers usually don't have credit elsewhere and aren't particularly careful about how they use it. They tend to run up large credit bills because they have never had credit cards before. In most cases, they quickly fall behind in their payments—giving us and the bank the legal right to double or sometimes even triple the interest rate on their card, plus late payment penalties. This aspect of our business is turning out to be much more profitable than selling clothes. In a real sense, the clothes on our rack are just lures to get customers into the store, where we can get them all signed up with charge cards.' "

"I thought at length that night about what my boss had said. It seemed like an unconscionable rip-off of people who didn't know how to handle credit and didn't know the financial bind they could get themselves into by overcharging their account and not paying their bills on time. I got my courage up and marched into my boss's office the next day to make my discomfort absolutely clear with his 'get-them-in-debt' policies toward customers. Without exactly indicting his integrity, I let him know that I didn't want to be part of any scheme that used a consumer's financial ignorance as the basis for the company's profits. My boss didn't like my protest and essentially told me to get with the program or leave. But I'm not a quitter, especially when I feel that I'm on the right side of things. I made an appointment with my boss's boss—the executive vice president of the company—and essentially delivered the same message about how our company was breaking faith with its customer base and ultimately risking legal ramifications. This time—thank goodness—the message found a receptive ear. He said he had not been fully aware of the implications of 'pushing charge cards as hard as we could onto every customer.' We agreed that consumer education was the missing element in the company's plans. He put me in charge of making sure that every customer who signed up for a charge card through us also went through a 15-minute 'full disclosure and training' session showing exactly what would happen if bills weren't paid and if credit balances grew too large. After seven months, two interesting things have happened. Our placement of credit cards in customers' hands have slowed a bit (about 15 percent), but our customer approval ratings have soared by more than 40 percent. Our customers praise us now for caring about their welfare as shoppers and looking out for their interests in difficult financial times. Sales are booming, largely from word of mouth from happy customers rather than from increased advertising. Even my original boss has come around to seeing the reality that being fair and honest with people—especially people who don't understand much about credit—is not only the right thing to do but is also the best thing to do for profitable companies."

Summing Up

The art of leadership involves in large part the art of delegation. Group members grow in loyalty to the organization and in abilities to perform by sharing vision, relationships, decision making, and responsibilities with the group leader. Small group leadership poses special challenges to the leader, who is usually well known by group members, easily accessible to them, and under some expectation that decision making will be based on group consensus. In attempting to lead apathetic or unwilling people, a leader may sometimes have to resort to using the authority given to him or her by the organization.

9

Leadership by Managing Conflict

GOALS

- understand the inevitability of conflict within teams
- observe ways in which a leader can deal with such conflict
- practice strategies and techniques for helping team members resolve conflict

Most experienced leaders accept the wisdom of the "90–10" rule: 90 percent of a leader's effort is spent dealing with 10 percent of his or her people. Like it or not, we all face the challenge of dealing successfully with the most problematic of those people—the "bad apples" who make school and work life miserable for those around them. We'll call them S.O.P.s: Sources of Pain.

THE S.O.P.

S.O.P.s can be found in every organization and profession. Above us in the pecking order may be the administrator, boss, or senior executive who isn't doing his or her job but who wants to tell us how to do ours. Next to us is the S.O.P. classmate or coworker who refuses to cooperate, understand, or even try. And below us may be one or more whining S.O.P.s who can't seem to accomplish even the simplest task without hand-holding. S.O.P.s can also be outsiders—sometimes our acquaintances or clients.

YOUR TURN

Without naming names, describe some of the actions and the influence of a "bad apple" with whom you have worked or served on a team. How did group members respond to such actions?

_____

_____

_____

_____

_____

_____

INSIGHT 48

Conflict among team members often stems from interpersonal misunderstandings and disrespect.

When Firing Isn't an Option

Assume for now (as leaders often must) that you can't afford to quit if you're working under an S.O.P.; that you can't get a transfer if you're working next to an S.O.P.; and that, for fear of legal action, college politics, or other reasons, you can't summarily fire an S.O.P. working for you. (Perhaps no paper trail yet exists to document a person's poor performance. Worse, a handful of neutral or mildly positive evaluations may already be on file for the person—the kind of evaluations you may have written in a hurry to avoid hassles and hurt feelings. In the workplace, these documents can be important evidence of wrongful termination in legal action against you if your S.O.P. is fired with undue haste.)

In short, you have to cope with your bad apple for the time being. How can you make the best of it for yourself and your organization?

Understanding Our Own Roles in the Problem

Without denying that our bad apple is...well, rotten to the core, we must nevertheless take responsibility for the subtle and not-so-subtle ways in which we aggravate an already bad situation. Consider, for example, how we usually picture the workplace drama of personalities. The majority of us, the "good guys," get along well—we're a happy family. The bad apple, as the social outcast, is seen as an aggressor who threatens the relatively passive majority, the "victims" of his misdeeds. We communicate this interpretation of the bad apple in the very language we use to describe him:

"Richard makes me so mad."

"Richard drives me crazy."

"Richard ruins my whole day."

But that interpretation of the bad apple at school or work overlooks what newsman Paul Harvey calls "the rest of the story." What are members of the happy family doing in response to the actions and attitudes of the bad apple? The usual answer is falsely innocent: "We didn't do *anything* to him. We were just minding our own business."

In fact, the drama of conflict between a bad apple and surrounding group members or workers involves both attack and counterattack. Understanding what we do *to* the bad apples in our midst is the first step in learning to how to deal with them successfully.

NATURAL REACTION 1: WE STRIP THE BAD APPLE   Stung by our latest encounter with a bad apple, we strip him or her of virtually all positive attributes. The coworker who nettles us is reduced to "that idiot—he or she's completely useless!" The boss who crosses us suddenly becomes "a jerk who always plays favorites." We're blinded to *any* redeeming qualities in the bad apple by the glare of hurt and anger. In so doing, we virtually guarantee that a bad situation will worsen.

YOUR TURN

Think more deeply about the individual you called to mind in the first "Your Turn" exercise in this chapter. Did group members tend to strip this individual of any positive attributes? If so, how?

_____

_____

_____

_____

_____

INSIGHT 49

The entire team plays a part in amplifying individual instances of conflict with a particular team member.

NATURAL REACTION 2: WE DEFAME THE BAD APPLE   Having stripped the problem employee of all positive qualities, we commit further interpersonal aggression by building consensus against the individual. Over coffee or lunch, we tell and retell our grievances to all who will listen. We inquire about their experiences with the bad apple, with the strong implication that we want to hear "the dirt." We dredge up past events involving the individual, sometimes rewriting history from years back to put him or her in as unfavorable a light as possible.

The net result of this group groan, unfortunately, is to blind us further to our own interests regarding the bad apple. We become more convinced than ever of the justice and wisdom of our strong emotional reactions. How could we be wrong when so many coworkers support our outrage?

Defaming the bad apple clouds our judgment and objectivity. Urged on by the cheerleaders we've invited to join our cause, we take unconsidered and unwise actions against the bad apple—actions that often cost us dearly in productivity, emotional wear and tear, employee morale, and legal entanglement.

YOUR TURN

Continue to think about the individual described in the "Your Turn" exercises so far in this chapter. Did group members try to build consensus against this member? If so, how?

_____

_____

_____

_____

INSIGHT 50

Groups have a tendency to gang up on individuals they identify as problem personalities.

NATURAL REACTION 3: WE EXPLAIN THE BAD APPLE   Faced with increasing interpersonal conflict, we tend to ascribe motives to the bad apple. Interestingly, we never ascribe reasonable or well-intentioned motives to the problem person; instead, we heap on any explanations that make the bad apple appear as narrow, self-seeking, vengeful, or stupid as possible.

By creating (and getting others to believe) our explanations regarding why the bad apple behaves as he or she does, we too easily fashion a monster from the cloth of our own emotional baggage. It's more helpful, and certainly more strategic, to begin with a blank slate in interpreting conflict with a bad apple in our organization. A leader is wise to say from the outset, "*I don't know* why Richard is acting this way."

This stance leaves us the flexibility to take an obvious but often overlooked step: *to ask the bad apple what motivates his or her actions.* Chances are at least 50–50 that the problem employee will tell us his or her side of the story. Understanding that background, we will be in a much better position as leaders to respond rationally, carefully, and perhaps even sympathetically.

YOUR TURN

As a final reflection on the individual described so far in this chapter's exercises, recall whether the group made up explanations for the person's behavior. What were those explanations? Did such explanations make conflict greater or less with the person?

_____

_____

_____

_____

INSIGHT 51

Groups cooperate to create a believable fiction for explaining the motives and actions of a problem personality. Usually, this fiction casts the offending individual negatively.

LEADERSHIP AND CONFLICT RESOLUTION: A THREE-STEP MODEL

If all human conflict could be resolved by three simple steps, we should each have these guidelines tattooed on our arms for ease of reference. In fact, most human conflict in the workplace and in our social lives is too complex to be whisked away by the application of a simple formula.

That being said, it can be helpful to look at three of the underlying principles by which conflict can be eased. These are offered not as automatic solutions but instead as areas for thoughtful reflection. We intend each of the steps in the following three-part model to help you understand the nature of the conflict at hand more deeply—and thus be more successful in dealing with it.

Step 1 Own your part in the conflict If a coworker comes up to you seething with anger over a perceived injustice of some kind, it's usually unproductive to dismiss the occurrence as "YP—Your Problem." Develop the courage and integrity to face up to your possible (if inadvertent) part in creating the conflict. Upon reflection, you may decide that you were entirely innocent and that the ranting person before you simply misunderstands. If this is the case, you've found your approach: explaining calmly and patiently why you're not guilty as charged.

On the other hand, upon reflection, you may have to admit that you did have some part in creating the conflict. Again, that reflection has provided your approach: facing up to what you said or did, perhaps apologizing if appropriate, and through words and actions, begin to convince the angry person of your true intentions. In many cases, the conflict at hand may stem from an entirely inaccurate interpretation of motives. The person thought you meant harm when in fact you didn't. But open-minded reflection will allow you to see how the person *might have come to that erroneous conclusion*— and will give you the opportunity (through reassurances, clarifications, and so forth) to help the person see your point of view.

Step 2 **Listen so long as you are not being abused** No one stands willingly in the dragon's breath, and we're not asking you to be the saint who listens while being "cussed out" or otherwise abused. In such cases (which, unfortunately, too often verge into physical abuse), you have every right to call a "time-out" and remove yourself from the situation, even when the dragon is your boss: "I understand that you're very angry, and I'm willing to have this conversation when you've calmed down. I'm not willing to be abused." (Exit stage right or left!)

But short of verbal abuse, it's wise on your part to hear the person out rather than trying to shut him or her down at the first sign of pique. You can even use probes to draw out the full story: "You're obviously quite upset. Tell me exactly what caused your strong feelings on this issue." "I don't blame you for being angry, but I do want to understand the whole picture. Start from the beginning." These kinds of inquiries demonstrate to the angry person that you are sincerely interested in getting to the root of the problem and not to suppress his or her feelings. In the process of probing, try to avoid "why" probes, such as "Why are you mad at me?" or "Why are you getting so upset?" These approaches are often taken as judgments, not expressions of caring or concern. When you say "why," the angry person hears "You're wrong to be acting this way."

Hearing out the full story gives you the opportunity to separate fact from fiction, rumor from reality, and personalities from actual occurrences. With all the facts before you, you have the best chance of piecing together a response and a solution that moves the conflict toward a solution.

Step 3 **Involve the angry person in the conflict resolution process** No matter how angry the person is as he or she stands red-faced before you, there's a good chance that he or she has some idea of how the conflict could or should be resolved. Getting the upset person to divulge that possible solution is a large part of ending conflict. Needless to say, what the angry person wants is not necessarily what you will be willing to give to end the problem. But you need the person's participation in the process of creating a solution as much as he or she needs your patience in listening to the whole rant. Again, nonjudgmental probes can help you ferret out the person's ideas about ending the conflict: "You've obviously spent a lot of time thinking about all this. Putting anger aside just for a moment, what do you think we could do together to find the right solution?" "You're giving me a good perspective on how you see this problem, and I don't blame you for being upset. What do you think would be a good first step toward a solution?"

If your image of a leader is a man or woman resolutely looking ahead, with followers loyally trailing behind, reverse your image. Turn the leader around so that he or she, even while walking ahead into the future, is facing his or her followers. That's the somewhat awkward but necessary posture that most real leaders experience. Most of their attention is devoted to their followers and their needs—sometimes peevish and petty, sometimes profound and difficult to resolve. A leader can't afford to let conflict fester unattended. When followers conclude that a leader doesn't care about their feelings, discontent spreads like a dangerous contagion that can quickly bring down the leader as well as the productivity of the group.

LANGUAGE THAT ENCOURAGES CONFLICT RESOLUTION

By avoiding the three natural reactions described earlier, you leave open the possibility of frank communication with the bad apple. But how do such problem-solving conversations begin? The following icebreakers have proven successful for many leaders eager to resolve rather than to fuel conflict.

- "Let's not play the blame game. Tell me how you see the problem."
- "I want to know your feelings about the situation and how you think we can get back on track."
- "I'm not asking for an apology. I do want to understand where you're coming from."
- "In your view, what can I do to help resolve the problem? What can you do?"

These and similar conversation starters move the focus away from accusation and toward honest disclosure and solution seeking.

YOUR TURN

Call to mind a time when you said something that helped to resolve conflict. What words did you use?

_____

_____

_____

_____

_____

_____

INSIGHT 52

Part of leadership skill in conflict resolution involves going beyond good intentions to practice actual phrases and sentences that can begin the healing process within the team.

LEARNING TO FIGHT THE FEELING

Finally, a leader who wants to cope successfully with a bad apple in the organization can achieve impressive results by *reversing* the three natural reactions described earlier. Instead of stripping the bad apple of all redeeming attributes, try to find positive characteristics or behaviors and build upon those. Instead of defaming the bad apple, mention something that he or she contributes to the organization—and make sure that the bad apple hears about it. Instead of explaining the motives of the bad apple negatively, withhold judgment until you've had a chance to hear all sides of the story.

The old cliché has it that one bad apple ruins the bunch. For the sake of the organization, if not the individual problem employee, it's in every leader's interest to deal with bad apples as calmly, humanely, and strategically as possible.

YOUR TURN

Focusing on a person's positive characteristics can be difficult when most evidence points to negative conclusions. Tell about a time when you chose to focus on a person's best points instead of his or her worst points. What was the result of your choice? How did things turn out?

_____

_____

_____

_____

_____

_____

INSIGHT 53

No team member is wholly without positive qualities. By focusing on those qualities, a leader can help resolve conflict without ignoring negative actions or personality traits that must be addressed.

WHEN LEADERSHIP FALTERS

In the same way that leaders evaluate and make recommendations to followers, so followers must sometimes judge the performance of their leader and even take action to change it. This process has been called "managing up"—finding ways to direct the efforts (or lack of effort) of the leader into more productive channels. Obviously such managing up comes with significant risks. The boss may interpret helpful observations and suggestions as impertinent interference or even insubordination. Those who attempt to manage up sometime find themselves looking for new employment.

Viewed positively, however, a shrewd leader has little to lose and everything to gain by letting his or her people know that he or she is open to constructive criticism and helpful advice. As one insurance executive in Chicago told us, "I would rather hear about my mistakes from my own people than later from my bosses." One form of loyalty to a leader, in fact, involves the courage and courtesy of telling the leader when he or she is about to step onto a land mine in one form or another.

Here are 10 common symptoms of leadership failure. Learn to watch for these symptoms and to make your leader aware of them before they metamorphose into full-blown business disasters:

1. An unusual attitude of isolation or withdrawal on the part of the leader: "He just doesn't talk to any of us anymore."
2. Continual expressions of discouragement and hopelessness: "If she doesn't think we have a chance of succeeding, why try?"
3. Repeated broken engagements, forgotten appointments, and altered schedules: "This meeting must not be very important. The boss has cancelled it three times."
4. Heightened temper as the leader's prime motivator and mode of communication: "I've never seen him like this. People are afraid to go into his office for fear of being shouted at."
5. Overt favoritism that subverts team morale: "He has decided that Alice walks on water and that the rest of us are pretty much worthless."
6. Lack of due diligence in the review of work product. "She used to read my reports like a hawk. Now she just hands them back to me without comment, if I get them back at all. Does she even care anymore?"
7. Signs of work stress played out as psychosomatic symptoms. "He couldn't come to work last week because of migraine headaches, and this week his stomach is acting up. The guy is falling apart."
8. Irrational exuberance over a single ill-founded or unproven idea: "She thinks all the problems we've been experienced can be resolved by an off-site retreat. I think she's putting too many eggs in one basket."
9. Ad hominem attacks at meetings and in interpersonal contacts: "He told Linda that she was long overdue for retirement right in front of her entire workgroup. She really felt humiliated."
10. Repeated focus on nonbusiness interests and activities: "All he can talk about is his new boat. I'm sure it's great, but do we have to hear about it at every meeting?"

LEADING IN THE FACE OF PERSONAL CRISIS

When a coworker or a group member faces a personal crisis, it affects everyone on the school or work team emotionally and professionally. But as much as we use the term *family* to describe relationships within our groups, we cannot and should not literally take on the personal responsibility for employees that a parent feels for a child. In a strict legal sense, the events of a group member's or employee's personal life aren't a leader's business, unless that person chooses to share those circumstances. Even in that case, personal information should not be solicited or pursued unless it has clear implications for work performance and is given voluntarily.

This is a long way of saying that leaders, managers, and other employees can't stand *in loco parentis* (in the role of parents)—and certainly not in the role of physician or psychologist—when it comes to the moods, inner struggles, and personal crises of their team members, subordinates, and coworkers. Although friendships develop easily and naturally in the workplace, there is always a healthful distance present ("we work together") that separates most school and work relationships from true family bonds and responsibilities.

What Leaders Can Do

Although leaders shouldn't play the work role of parent, amateur shrink, or priest, rabbi, or minister, they can help prevent personal tragedy and school or workplace violence in at least three ways.

1. *Monitor the work group for psychological violence, particularly in the forms of bullying, ostracizing, and painful teasing.* When group members or employees select a "goat" to persecute in subtle and not-so-subtle ways, they are setting the stage for an outburst of some kind from the persecuted person, often with violence that is either self-directed or aimed toward coworkers or management. When you discover psychologically harmful or violent games being played out in your school or workplace, get involved immediately. Talk in depth with all parties and put "teeth" in your efforts to resolve the situation by linking employee behavior to your reward system. Break up coworkers who demonstrate explosive interpersonal chemistry by physically separating their work spaces, shifts, and opportunities for interaction.

YOUR TURN

Describe an occasion when you observed bullying taking place. Tell what you did or, by hindsight, what you could have done to manage such conflict.

_____

_____

_____

_____

_____

INSIGHT 54

Psychological violence is rampant in the workplace. It compromises productivity, team morale, and leadership effectiveness.

2. *Take offhand remarks, jests, and innuendo seriously when such remarks have to do with "ending it all," "they will pay for this," "they don't know who they're messing with," or similar portents of violent action.* Involve your college or company counselor (or find such a person through your employee assistance program) in immediate intervention. You may discover that a joke was just that—a joke about "blowing my brains out" and nothing more. But take the statistics seriously: among the millions of clinically depressed people in America, about one-third of those who threaten suicide will eventually attempt it. And, perhaps more tragically, half of that number will have seen their personal physician or psychologist within a month of the suicide attempt. Words about killing oneself—or others—no longer can be taken merely as idle chatter or the venting of frustration in the workplace.

YOUR TURN

What language do college students and young employees typically use to convey emotional upset, exhaustion, or depression? List as many of these phrases as come to mind.

_____

_____

_____

_____

_____

_____

INSIGHT 54

Leaders have a responsibility to act immediately on expressed or implied threats of violence to team members.

3. *Watch for changes in work performance that are entirely out of character for the group member involved.* Jane, let's say, has been an on-time, on-task performer all year on your team or in your office. Suddenly, she begins to miss deadlines,

show resentment for supervision, and turn in low-quality work. As the leader of her group, you have the obligation to ask her (privately, in a nonthreatening environment) just what is going on. Stick to what you have observed in the school or work environment, not what you surmise about her personal life. Listen to what she says—and doesn't say. Often a group member's sighs, long pauses, averted eyes, and downcast looks and posture can tell quite a different story from her overt words: "I've just been kind of blue. It's nothing."

Although you should not probe beyond the appropriate limits of the leader–team member relationship, you certainly can and should refer a troubled group member to a health professional or a college or company counselor. There should be no stigma attached to such a referral. As a leader, you are simply exercising due diligence in doing your part to defuse potentially harmful circumstances.

YOUR TURN

Describe a time when the performance of a team member or coworker "fell apart." What caused the change? What could the leader have done to manage the situation more successfully?

_____

_____

_____

_____

_____

_____

INSIGHT 56

Leaders should not turn a blind eye to obvious changes in a team member's attitudes or performance. These changes may indicate deep-seated problems that will eventually affect the team, its leader, and the organization.

Admittedly, the chances that Jane, Jim, or Juan will return to your group meeting with a shotgun are slight indeed. But the chances are much greater that emotionally distressed employees will blow up unexpectedly at you, another group member or coworker, or a client; quit without notice or "check out" from their tasks and responsibilities by doing only the minimum required; become involved in school or workplace vandalism or theft; or increase group tension to the breaking point by their displays of moodiness and temper. As a leader, you can't make your group members happy in their personal lives. But you can act each day to make sure that your members' personal upsets and emotional problems don't threaten the productivity or safety of your school or workplace.

PREVENTING BURNOUT FOR TEAM MEMBERS

For those who have repetitive, low-pay, and low-prestige jobs, the phenomenon of burnout is no mystery. As any of us might, they become discouraged over time by their dim prospects. They often react by showing up late, abusing sick leave, wearing their lackluster attitude on their sleeves, and working at a snail's pace.

But what about your brightest and best? Burnout is most devastating to an organization of any kind—and most difficult to understand—when it strikes your top performers and workforce leaders, or perhaps even you yourself. These people have everything to live and work for in the organization: great reputations, excellent prospects, good pay, attractive promotion possibilities, comfortable work conditions, and interesting job assignments.

So what's the problem? This portion of our discussion of conflict investigates four reasons why your brightest and best may be fading in morale and productivity even as you read this book. For each reason, you will find here a suggested solution you can begin using today to rekindle the fire in the belly for achievement and excellence among your top people.

REASON 1: "I JUST CAN'T PUSH THIS HARD ANYMORE."   Your best team members or employees have probably been setting high goals for themselves throughout their lives. They worked hard for good grades throughout school. They pushed themselves to the limit in sports programs. They arrived early, stayed late, and worked intensely and well in their first job experiences. And now, in your organization, they've hit the wall. They are exhausted not by prolonged discouragement but instead by its opposite: the sustained excitement and adrenalin levels of their challenging positions.

YOUR TURN

Describe a time when you observed a talented individual "hit the wall" in terms of personal stamina. How did that person indicate his or her problem? How did things turn out?

_____

_____

_____

_____

_____

_____

INSIGHT 57

Leaders monitor for signs of burnout because they value the well-being and continued contributions of team members.

The mini-sabbatical solution.   High-achieving team members or employees usually can't be given slow-go work assignments to let them rest up and refresh their energies. Such assignments would be seen by these employees and their peers not as a perk for performance but as a demotion of sorts, even if their pay did not change. Sun Microsystems, IBM, Cisco Systems, and other computer companies have led the way in offering short-term sabbaticals (not additional vacation time) to employees who have given their all to the job and are understandably near the breaking point. These mini-sabbaticals typically last two to six weeks. The employee in question goes off-site to pursue personal research, academic seminars, professional continuing education, or another activity that, in Jung's phrase, "waters the tree"—that is, refreshes the physical and psychological sources of motivation and creativity.

Are such mini-sabbaticals expensive to the organization? Not when you compare their cost to the much greater expense of losing a key employee and then going through the rehiring and training process for a replacement. The American Management Association estimates that replacing a midlevel manager costs, on average, about one year's salary for that individual. Do the math yourself: a lost key employee means lost productivity, new advertising, and perhaps headhunter expenses to attract candidates; the enormous investment of executive time in choosing a replacement; and, finally, the hidden but significant costs involved in bringing that new individual up to speed in your organization. By contrast, a mini-sabbatical may involve your expenditure of just a few weeks' wages—with the upside potential that the star employee will return to burn brightly with newfound skills, energy, and ideas instead of burning out.

YOUR TURN

Write about a time when you took a valuable "time out" from school or work activities. What did you do during this time off? In what ways did your period away from school or work responsibilities influence your attitudes and productivity once you returned to school or work?

_____

_____

_____

_____

_____

_____

INSIGHT 58

"Burn-out" can strike even the most dedicated leader or group member. Learn to spot the symptoms of burn-out early, then deal with them in ways that you know will restore your sense of healthfulness and work/life balance.

REASON 2: "I'VE REACHED MY POTENTIAL HERE; THERE'S NOTHING TO STRIVE FOR."   Alexander the Great wept when he was informed by his captains that there were no more countries to conquer. Highly talented individuals usually have their own agendas (often unexpressed to you) as to what they want to accomplish by a chronological age (their 30s, 40s, or 50s) or by comparison with a parent, friend, or sibling ("where my dad was after five years on the job"). No matter how much deserved praise you heap on them, these key team members or employees feel let down when the major organizational mountains have been successfully scaled. They respond either by looking for new employment elsewhere or by "turning off" and checking out as performers in your organization.

YOUR TURN

Describe a time when you felt bored by your role on a team or by your participation on a project. How did you express your feelings? Did you resolve the problem?

_____

_____

_____

_____

_____

_____

INSIGHT 59

Team members need appropriate challenges to remain interested and involved in the work and goals of the team.

The executive involvement solution.   To keep work life interesting and challenging for your brightest and best, invent ways to bring them into your counsel as organizational architects and decision makers. Some leaders form an "executive council" made up of their most talented people. This council meets, often at attractive off-site locations, to assess future opportunities and vulnerabilities for the organization, to strategize for serving clients and other stakeholders more effectively and profitably, and to advise managers and supervisors on how to get the most from the workforce while building morale and team spirit. When talented people are brought into the highest levels of creative planning and decision making, they have a reason to keep their own skills sharp and to resist burnout.

REASON 3: "IT'S EVERYTHING ELSE GOING ON IN MY LIFE RIGHT NOW." The demographics of the Sandwich Generation (your team members between the ages of 21 and 55 or older) reveal that many have young children to raise at the same time that they have primary financial and personal responsibility for elderly parents. Daughters, in fact, are 11 times more likely than sons to serve as primary caregivers for aging parents. The demands of being "soccer mom" while simultaneously being on daily or hourly call for the pains, panics, and prescriptions of grandma and grandpa take their toll on even the most giving and responsible person. When a heavy workload falls on top of heavy family commitments, the result can be crushing. Productivity plummets, absenteeism increases, and burnout becomes a way of work life for the person—in effect, a week-to-week survival mechanism—instead of a rare "blah day."

YOUR TURN

List several factors in your day-to-day life that compete for your energy and attention in relation to your responsibilities on a school or work team. How do you balance your personal life and your work life?

_____

_____

_____

_____

_____

INSIGHT 60

Leaders cannot pretend that team members have no lives outside of work. Although a leader cannot always make adjustments for such life situations, he or she must be flexible in helping team members avoid impossible pressures and conflicting obligations.

The kincare solution.   As chronicled each year in *Working Woman's* list of family-friendly companies, organizations can ease the burnout-inducing burdens of family responsibilities without breaking the budget by installing so-called cafeteria benefits plans. With a bit of creative research and planning by your HR staff, employees can be given a menu of benefit choices from which to select programs that will help them meet their family or other personal responsibilities and get back to productive work. In a school environment, an on-site child-care center or referral network can serve the same ends. Among such menu items in typical cafeteria benefits plans are resource and referral services for child and elder care, on- or off-site child-care or elder-care facilities (often shared with other area companies), provision for sick-child visitation and day care by a medically trained caregiver, substance abuse assistance, and alternative work scheduling (including compressed workweeks, flextime, telecommuting, and so forth).

YOUR TURN

Describe a school or work situation in which you or someone you know had difficulty completing assigned work and meeting deadlines due to pressing family obligations. How did the instructor or boss handle the situation? Did he or she even know? In the circumstance you have described, what kinds of adaptive solutions could have been applied without compromising the overall goal of meeting school or work goals? Be as specific as possible.

_____

_____

_____

_____

_____

_____

INSIGHT 61

A "culture of health" in an organization makes sure that members do not drive themselves (or be driven) beyond their physical and emotional limits.

REASON 4: "I DON'T KNOW WHAT IT IS. I'M JUST DEEP-DOWN TIRED."   The American Medical Association reports that fatigue and depression are among the top complaints that bring patients to physicians. Especially for employees approaching the real or imagined doldrums of a midlife crisis, sensations of lost energy, stamina, or ambition can easily be extrapolated into self-authenticating "proof" of burnout. Fortunately, we inhabit an era where chronic fatigue syndrome and the broad range of depression-induced symptoms are taken seriously by physicians. New pharmacological and psychological tools have proven extraordinarily successful for resolving or relieving these problems.

The caring organization solution.   Traditionally, leaders and employers have hesitated to pry into a team member's or worker's health or emotional circumstances. "Job performance is all that counts," such organizations proclaimed. Unfortunately, performance often suffered precisely because the organization could not help when its members experienced illness in its myriad forms.

Without crossing obvious lines of propriety, you can lead your organization in encouraging a "culture of health." It works like this: from the top down, each member of the organization is urged to take his or her physical and emotional well-being seriously. The organization can provide stress-reduction seminars; exercise and weight-reduction sessions; "healthy-heart" menus in the food facility; smoking cessation programs and incentives; and, in general, an atmosphere of openness and sharing where personal feelings and physical problems are concerned.

The Americans with Disabilities Act (ADA) requires "reasonable accommodation" for workers with disabilities. Why not extend that logic in your organization to all your employees? Accommodation can be as simple as understanding that John suffers occasionally from migraine headaches and may have to take short breaks from work, or that a group of exercising employees needs an additional 15 minutes at lunch twice a week to complete their regimen, or that a smoke-free workplace, including restrooms, will help your many employees who are trying hard to break the habit.

YOUR TURN

List several mental and physical health supports that could be provided for a team on which you now serve or have served in the past.

_____

_____

_____

_____

_____

_____

These easily affordable solutions let employees know that the company does not want them to hide personally distressing symptoms of burnout until the 11th hour. The organization that encourages consciousness of physical and emotional health reaps the benefit of employees more likely to experience such health.

INSIGHT 62

Leaders commit to the welfare of their team members and do what they can to promote a healthy, enjoyable work environment.

Burnout in all its forms costs American corporations billions of dollars each year in lost productivity, rapid turnover, careless mistakes, and failed leadership. To start combating burnout in your organization, face up to the strong possibility that some of your brightest and best may now be experiencing these symptoms with or without your knowledge. Take immediate steps as a leader to understand what they are going through; then work together to find a solution (perhaps one contained in this chapter) to make work inspiring and even fun again.

MEET A LEADER

Brent W.
A Political Organizer with Responsibility for College Campuses.

"My leadership approach can be stated quite simply: I get others to take over leadership on their campus as quickly as possible. With responsibility for 18 campuses on the West Coast, I simply can't attend student political meetings in person very often. So I do my best to follow a three-step process in my job. First, I try to inspire local leaders and let them know they have access to me for advice and resources. Second, I spend some time training these leaders on the specific strategies and techniques they can use to attract other students to their organization on campus. Finally, I monitor results at each campus (in terms of number of students involved, type of activities, and nature of any obstacles or barriers encountered) and try to help wherever possible."

"The idea of giving up primary leadership responsibility was difficult for me at first. I wanted to be, in effect, the big cheese and have my lieutenants at each of my campuses. I thought I could simply send instructions to these people, who then would carry out my wishes within their local organizations. I quickly learned that this kind of 'command and control' approach to leadership didn't work well with a variety of campus cultures, different personalities among campus leaders, and challenges on the 18 campuses that had less in common than I could have imagined. I found that I had to rely on the energy, good sense, and adaptive leadership style of each campus leader rather than impose my own approach. When I visit campuses now, I find myself doing much more listening than talking. Local campus leaders are eager to let me know what they are trying, how they are gathering support, and what they are doing to overcome problems. Sometimes I have specific suggestions that can help, but often I find myself just cheering these individuals on and telling them to keep up the good work. When I look back, I used to think of leadership as being at the head of the parade. Now I understand that, at least in my job, it's more like jumping around to other marchers in the parade to see if I can help out in any way. I thought I needed to inspire them; it turns out that, on most days, they end up inspiring me."

Summing Up

Conflict occurs in virtually all human groups and organizations. A leader must manage such conflict successfully if the team is to achieve its goals, whether in college or work life. Too often, conflict is blamed on specific individuals without any examination of the group's role in perpetuating and aggravating such tension. A leader can help the group consider its own motives and actions as a starting place for dealing with the bad apple.

In conflict involving personal crisis, the leader has a crucial role in acting within legal limits to intervene in any instances of psychological or physical violence in the school or workplace. Such intervention also applies to instances of actual or impending burnout among stressed team members. A three-step model for conflict resolution involves owning one's own part in the conflict, listening to facts and feelings, and engaging all parties in the process of resolution.

10

Leadership by Supporting and Empowering Participation

GOALS

- learn ways to lead and encourage more participative meetings
- use leadership skills to improve the quality of thinking in organizations
- lead by monitoring and nurturing the knowledge required for team performance

We all have attended meetings that were disorganized, poorly led, boring, and therefore unproductive. We walk away feeling that our time has been wasted. The meeting leader, we may feel, is largely to blame for the failure of the meeting. The leader could have distributed an orderly agenda, directed the traffic of discussion, focused the attention of the group on its goals, and taken other steps to ensure a meaningful meeting. We may also blame the meeting participants. They could have listened more carefully to one another, kept their comments concise and on target, and worked together to reach good decisions. This chapter shows leaders how to master meeting skills so that these gatherings achieve their goals.

PARTICIPATION IN MEETINGS

Meetings are the most obvious arena for increased participation—both in quality and in quantity—by team members. How does a leader get team members to give their best effort to such occasions?

To approach an answer, think for a moment about the nature of team meetings. By any estimate, these get-togethers are an expensive habit for any organization. You're calling people away from their day-to-day tasks to . . . well, talk. At your next meeting, add up what the company is spending in prorated salary or hourly wages to have the participants sitting around a table for a couple of hours—and then ask where the meeting earned its keep. It's not uncommon to discover $1,000 meetings called to deal with a $100 problem.

YOUR TURN

Call to mind a recent meeting you attended. What went right and what went wrong?

_____

_____

_____

_____

_____

_____

_____

Better meetings begin by asking an obvious question: *do we really need to meet?* If a personal conversation, phone call, or e-mail to a few people can settle a matter, there's no good reason to convene the troops and waste most of the morning or afternoon. The leader of every meeting should be able to say at the beginning of a meeting exactly why the gathering is necessary and what needs to be accomplished.

INSIGHT 63

Team members can participate best in meetings that are necessary.

If a meeting is required, make sure that the right people—and only the right people—are asked to attend. We've all had the annoying experience of sitting in a bad meeting and asking ourselves, "Why am I here?" That question is particularly frustrating when real work is piling up on our desks. Management sage Peter Drucker put the matter wryly: "We can meet or we can work. We can't do both at the same time."

A Checklist for Meeting Leaders

Here are 10 quick questions that can help a meeting leader run a productive, cost-effective meeting.

1. Did I send out an agenda with enough advance notice so that people could put the meeting on their calendars?
2. Did I let people know what materials to bring along to the meeting and how to prepare for discussion?
3. Did I start and end the meeting on time? (Everyone loves a meeting leader who starts a 9 A.M. to 10:30 A.M. meeting precisely at 9 A.M. and concludes it no later than 10:30 A.M. unless the group wants to extend the meeting time.)
4. Did I begin the meeting by clearly stating its main purpose(s) and setting goals for what the meeting can accomplish?
5. Did I remember that God gave me two ears and one mouth—and that they should be used in that proportion? (Meeting leaders need to avoid lecturing.)
6. Did I draw all participants into discussion ("Linda, give us your perspective") as a way of preventing the big mouths from dominating?
7. Did I focus discussion ("Let's make sure we're clear on this point") to bring the group back from distractions?
8. Did I work for consensus rather than "us versus them" votes?
9. Did I conclude the meeting by summing up what was decided and recapping any individual assignments or deadlines?
10. Did I make sure that accurate minutes of meeting were distributed within a day or two after the meeting?

YOUR TURN

Think about a meeting you have led. Did you ignore any of the 10 points listed earlier? If so, which ones? How would the meeting have been more successful if these points had been followed?

_____

_____

_____

_____

_____

_____

INSIGHT 64

Successful leadership of meetings rests primarily on the leader's planning efforts to help meeting participants participate fully.

The Temptations of Leading Meetings

Some leaders are guilty of the "drama or trauma" approach to meetings. With a flair for the dramatic, the Star Leader assembles the troops merely as an audience to watch him or her rant, bluster, and moan. Or, the Star Leader calls a meeting for the purpose of trauma—that is, the public humiliation of the guilty and the blessing of the saints. Such psychodrama may help the Star Leader work out his or her issues, but it does little to build the team, inspire achievement, or get work done.

Other meeting leaders are guilty of the "red, white, and blue" options for company meetings. Red meetings are called (usually with five minutes' notice) when the boss is fit to be tied and wants to scream at people. These are the meetings in which there is usually more heat than light.

White meetings are the neutral, ho-hum meetings that were entered on the leader's calendar months in advance. Why hold the Monday meeting? Because it's Monday, of course. We always meet on Monday morning (even when there's little reason to do so).

Blue meetings are called when the bored or isolated leader feels "it would just be good to get together." These are the Lonesome Guy meetings, which have no particular agenda and simply plod on, sometimes for hours, all in the name of "touching base with one another" and "sharing." Some companies save time and money by getting the Blue Leader a cat.

YOUR TURN

Call to mind a meeting that seemed to be more about the meeting leader and his or her feelings than about any specific agenda. What were your feelings about the meeting?

_____

_____

_____

_____

_____

INSIGHT 65

Meetings are an organizational event and expense, not a showcase for the leader's needs or feelings.

Expanded Roles for Meeting Participants

The responsibility for better meetings rests on participants as well as leaders. Bad meetings can often be blamed on participants who arrive late, conduct sidebar conversations throughout the meeting, pop in and out to handle phone calls, or simply sit silent while others actively participate in the meeting.

At root, such participants have settled on a narrow set of roles they are determined to play out in each meeting they attend. John the Objector will begin each of his comments with "But..." Ida the Idea person will ignore previous discussion to offer "a new way of looking at things." Sam the Cynic will mutter "I just don't think we're making any progress." Coleen the Closer will insist that the group "just decide—we've wasted enough time talking."

When such participants stick to their standard roles, it's no wonder that meetings become yawners. Just by looking at the list of attendees, you can predict approximately who will say what and how the meeting will devolve into chat or conflict. Such predictable meetings are the death of creativity in companies—a cul-de-sac, as one writer put it, "into which ideas are lured to be quietly strangled."

To avoid such stagnation, meeting participants should challenge themselves to take on at least three or four roles that they don't habitually use in meetings. This fresh-faced approach to meeting participation can enliven discussion, resolve old conflicts, and make meetings a stimulating part of the workday. Here's a list of meeting roles from which new roles can be selected.

- Idea person (Here's an idea...)
- Expander (Yes, and that also means...)
- Associator (I agree with _____ because...)
- Objector (I object because...)
- Devil's advocate (I don't necessarily object, but let me play out a contrary idea...)
- Complimenter (I think _____ deserves a lot of credit or praise because...)
- Bridge builder (Let's put some of the group's ideas together... for example...)
- Consensus seeker (So let's pause for a moment. Are we all in agreement that...)
- Sect seeker (Some of us don't feel that way. Do you want to hear from the minority?)
- Closer (Let's at least make a decision on this, then we can move on.)
- Evaluator (So far I think we've done a good job dealing with...)
- Personalizer (I can just tell you how I feel...)
- Criticizer (I don't think we're getting to the real issues...)
- Peacemaker (I'm sure we are all trying our best to seek solutions here...)
- Summarizer (Let me stop everyone for a minute so I can sum up what's been said so far...)
- Questioner (Tell me why you feel so strongly about that point.)
- Motive assassin (You're taking that position because it helps you...)
- Emotion meter (Here's the feeling I'm getting from this discussion...)
- Derailer (This may be way off track, but...)
- Authoritarian (Here's the way it is...)
- Submissive (I guess you're right. I didn't see it that way, but you're probably right.)

- Goal keeper (This talk is fine, but where does it lead? What are we trying to decide?)
- Divider (We basically have two separate camps here. One says...)
- Attacker (That's entirely wrong. I don't think you have any evidence to support your point.)
- Defender (I think we're all being to hard on _____. He's only saying that...)

YOUR TURN

Which of the roles listed earlier do you tend to use regularly? List two or three that you seldom use: then make plans to try out those new roles at the next meeting you attend.

_____

_____

_____

_____

_____

_____

INSIGHT 66

Meeting participants can too easily fall into the rut of expected behaviors. Meetings come alive when participants surprise one another by their range of discussion skills and options.

No meeting participant, of course, plays all or even most of these roles. The point is simply that most of us are in a rut when it comes to the standard roles we play over and over in meetings. We can each do our part to make meetings more productive—and, yes, more fun—by making our moves less predictable in the chess game of discussion. New roles wake other people up to what we're saying.

How do you get participants to develop these new discussion options and skills? Probably the best way is to devote a training meeting to the topic of better meetings. Two excellent videos to support such training are "Meetings, Bloody Meetings" and "More Bloody Meetings," both starring John Cleese (VideoArts Productions).

The Promised Land

When meeting leaders get their act together and meeting participants take on a few new roles, meetings can begin to serve their intended function in business life: a brief gathering where issues are examined fairly, debate is conducted energetically but respectfully, and decisions are reached that lead to worthwhile action. That's a meeting we would all like to attend.

DISTRIBUTED LEADERSHIP

Imagine a fishnet lying open on the ground. Wherever two strings of the net intersect, you can pinch that spot with your fingers and lift it upward. If that high spot in the net is symbolically viewed as the emergence of leadership, then the possibilities for "distributed leadership" become almost limitless in the total organization (or "fishnet").

Imagine, further, that top managers within organizations thought of their workforce as this kind of fishnet—an array of talented people where leaders could emerge at a moment's notice to deal with a crisis or opportunity, but then also settle back into "followership" as easily as the fishnet falls back into its original place once you open your fingers. In this kind of organization, people don't "climb the ladder" because the pattern and expectations for leadership are quite different: people watch for opportunities to lead because they are *called to do so by their skill and by the moment,* not because they are on an upward organizational escalator of some kind rising higher only through seniority, favoritism, or other force of advancement.

The fishnet organization has the advantage of being able to call of any of its members to rise to leadership service, even on a temporary basis. The traditional organization, by contrast, has difficulty asking the rank and file to perform leadership responsibilities:

"That's not in my job description" comes the standard reply. Organizational members who have been trained to think of themselves only and always as followers, not leaders, will stay true to form, waiting for "someone above" to give the order, make the decision, or provide instructions before acting.

LEADING TEAM MEMBERS TO THINK WELL

"One member of our team seems to have trouble . . . well, *thinking.* She can follow directions well, but when she has to solve a problem by herself we never know what to expect."

This approximate complaint comes to every leader's attention sooner or later. Thinking outside the box can help the company, but thinking outside city limits is a drag on all concerned. We joke about some coworkers having "one taco short of a combination plate." But it's no joke when we have to redo their work or, worse, when clients suffer the results of their incompetence.

YOUR TURN

How does a poor thinker affect the work of a team? What can the team do to help the poor thinker improve his or her intellectual skills?

_____

_____

_____

_____

_____

_____

INSIGHT 67

Team members who appear to have difficulty making sense can improve over time through training. Making one's point in a logical, well-supported way is a learned skill, not a birthright.

Spotting the Poor Thinker

People who have difficulty connecting the dots of an idea reveal themselves in at least three workplace arenas.

PARTICIPATION IN MEETINGS   The poor thinker doesn't track well with the flow of conversation and debate in meetings. He or she pops up with comments that cause other meeting participants to pause dumbfounded and silently ask themselves, "What was that all about?" The poor thinker often complains after the meeting that "no one responded to my idea" or "no one really listened to me." Out of politeness, coworkers usually just nod or shrug their shoulders—even when they are dying to say, "You don't make any sense!"

WRITING E-MAILS, LETTERS, AND MEMOS   The poor thinker gets by as long as he or she can copy model messages (or even cut and paste them) from company boiler-plate text. But watch out when an original message is required. Writing that requires the spark of individual intelligence is a virtual litmus test for the poor thinker. Fragments of ideas spill onto the page or screen in seemingly random order, connected not by logic but by a smokescreen of phrases, such as "as you know" and "first and foremost."

TELEPHONE AND OTHER ELECTRONIC CONTACT   The poor thinker ends up frustrating almost every caller with whom he or she has contact. Instead of listening thoroughly to the problem or request at hand, the poor thinker grabs at a single word or phrase and then proceeds to derail the conversation by irrelevant "yada yada yada." When the caller tries to repeat the real message, the poor thinker often gets snippy: "I already answered that, but I will repeat myself if you didn't hear me the first time." These calls inevitably bounce over as extra work for the supervisor or manager, who has to pick up the broken pieces of the conversation and repair the business relationship. In many cases, the client gives up entirely on the communication and seeks a new business relationship.

YOUR TURN

Call to mind a poor thinker with whom you have served or whom you have led on a school or work team. Why do you think he or she had difficulty understanding the purposes, techniques, and work habits of the rest of the group? In your opinion, could training have made a difference in this individual's performance? If so, briefly describe the kind of training that you feel would have been most effective. If not, tell how you think the problem of the poor thinker should be handled.

_____

_____

_____

_____

_____

_____

INSIGHT 68

When leaders encounter poor thinkers, the first step toward dealing with this problem is understanding its cause(s).

Decision Time: Develop or Dump the Poor Thinker

It's one of the illusions of youth that managers simply fire everyone who doesn't measure up to high work standards. In reality, especially in a tight labor market, a poor thinker who nevertheless knows the ropes of your operation may not be on your short list for "career adjustment." By investing training time and money in such individuals, you can earn an ongoing dividend of better performance and productivity from previous noncontributors. Here's a training and development regimen geared to the needs of many poor thinkers—perhaps including those in your workplace.

1. *Never label the individual overtly or covertly.* In performance evaluations, describe behaviors rather than attaching derogatory terms or names. Pay particular attention to the words you use about the individual in hallway or supposedly confidential conversation with others. If the poor thinker comes to think of himself or herself as slow-witted or obtuse, those conceptions become self-fulfilling prophecies. Instead, continually remind the individual of the importance of his or her job responsibilities and challenges. Breed professionalism by expecting it, even in the face of contrary evidence.

2. *Put the poor thinker into a regular, if ad hoc, training program that focuses on improved problem solving.* For example, each week or so write up a few sentences describing a typical business problem. Ask the individual to come up with a good solution to the problem; then meet with him or her to discuss how judgments and decisions were reached. (If the individuals feel singled out for such training, they have passed at least one reality check. They *are* being singled out, although the rest of the office does not need to know about it.)

3. *Help the poor thinker isolate his or her most typical thinking errors.* Following are some common ones.
   - *Circular thinking*—a rephrased idea takes the place of an explanation. For example, "Accurate 'hit' reports are necessary to provide precise measure of visits to a site." No kidding. A rose is a rose is a rose.
   - *False cause*—attributing a result to the order of events in time rather than to their causal relationship. For example: "We hired the new secretary last month and now I can't find the disk I'm looking for." Note that both statements are true: we did hire the new secretary last month (Event A), and the desired disk can't be found (Event B). But Event A did not necessarily cause Event B.
   - *Straw man*—reducing a complex problem to a surface symptom and then dealing only with that symptom. For example: "The proposed solution for Viewcrest Associates depends on how well Sam gets along with their vice president for MIS." Poor thinkers are always surprised when their straw man (in this case, Sam's interpersonal skills) turn out to be only one piece in a complex puzzle.
   - *Ad hominem explanations*—accounting for events solely on the basis of personal attributes and feelings. For example: "I've worked with Jenkins before, and he's a real jerk. Don't go out of your way to provide any extra services to him." Poor thinkers make quick judgments about individuals, then justify their behavior on the basis of those judgments, however incomplete or inaccurate.

4. *Praise the poor thinker when he or she makes meaningful comments in meetings, writes a good letter or memo, or handles a telephone contact well.* Such praise does not have to be patronizing. In a meeting, for example, it's enough simply to say, "Joe is making a good point" or "Alice, that's an interesting

---

YOUR TURN

Are you prone to making any of the logical errors described earlier? If so, which ones? If not, describe any difficulties you do face from time to time in making your point clearly and persuasively.

_____

_____

_____

_____

_____

_____

---

perspective. Tell us more about it." Praise has a wonderful way of not only buoying the motivation of workers but also helping them grasp in specific ways the kinds of work behaviors expected of them.

Let's not underestimate the problem of developing the poor thinker. It's a task that requires tact, patience, and insight. Even after months of effort on your part, you may not end up with an office Einstein. But you may well have tamed the Frankenstein who previously derailed your meetings, ruined your correspondence, and terrorized your telephone or Internet contacts.

INSIGHT 69

Leaders should look upon improvement in thinking as a practical training goal for team members, not as an impossible task that some school should have handled.

LEADING BY SUPPORTING TEAM KNOWLEDGE

Here's an interesting situation faced by a leader in the insurance industry: "One of our veteran employees—I'll call her Helen—resigned last week to take a better position with another company. Before she left, she took time to write down a list of tips, suggestions, and shortcuts for her replacement. It amazed me to see how much practical knowledge of the business she had in her head—and how much she has now taken to our competitor."

Employees like Helen are walking repositories of what we can call "embedded" knowledge. From her 20-plus years in the company, she has come to know techniques, tricks of the trade, and streamlined procedures that allow her to work smart (and perhaps hard, as well). But all that knowledge is in Helen's head, just as the knowledge to calculate large sums is embedded in a computer processing chip.

In fact, as you look around your firm or work group, you may be surprised to see how much vital company and industry knowledge is locked up in this embedded form. The knowledge contained in your organization's operations manuals, procedural guidelines, training books, chalk talks, executive memos, and all the rest doesn't add up to even a small percentage of the knowledge stored inside the heads of your team members and employees, particularly your most experienced ones.

So what? The previous century saw companies locked in a struggle to *outdo* one another. The new century challenges companies, especially information-based companies, to *out-know* one another. In earlier times, capacity for production guaranteed success; today, capacity for gaining and applying knowledge turns out to be the brass ring that lets you go around again.

If all that sounds like idealistic mumbo-jumbo (or "where the rubber meets the sky"), consider this practical translation. Every Helen who packs up her desk and walks out of your company carries a piece of your knowledge asset base with her. You usually can't prevent her from using her expertise elsewhere, even in direct competition with you. But you can structure your organization so that valuable knowledge remains with you when valuable people leave the company. Here's how:

1. *Perform a knowledge inventory.* By whatever notes or categorization you find most useful, write down *what* your organization needs to move profitably forward and *where* that knowledge now resides.

2. *If you find that your core knowledge assets are located primarily in written form or in software of some kind, test the transferability of such "external knowledge" to the heads of your people—that is, to where it will do some good for the company.* Do you have effective training programs in place that can bring new people up to speed quickly and reliably? Can your training programs or other knowledge-injection techniques respond quickly when the needs of the marketplace change or when new technologies or legal requirements pop up?

3. *If, on the other hand, you find that your core knowledge assets reside primarily in people, assess the vulnerability of such knowledge.* Would the retirement or resignation of a few key people leave you stuck in a knowledge gap? If so, your task should be to make "internal" knowledge (the stuff in Helen's head) as globally available to your company as possible. Even if Helen cannot write down all that she knows (probably a prodigious task), perhaps you can involve her in mentoring a "shadow" employee who is still learning the ropes. Or, you can lend Helen temporarily to your training group so that she can help to create a training curriculum focused on the knowledge that matters most.

4. *Commit to making knowledge inventories and knowledge acquisition a regular part of your business strategy, not a once-a-year ritual.* Along with the perpetual manager's question "How are we doing?" add a new question to your daily checklist: "What do we know and need to know?" Yesterday's knowledge and knowledge-gaining techniques just won't keep the lights on in a settlement-services environment demanding more economy, more accuracy, more reliability, more quality, and above all more speed.

YOUR TURN

Have you ever performed a knowledge inventory as described earlier? Give your opinion of whether such an inventory would be useful for a team or work group of which you are now a member.

_____

_____

_____

_____

_____

INSIGHT 70

Modern teams are typically made up of knowledge workers whose competitive advantage lies in their combined ability to out-know other groups. Therefore, the knowledge resources of the team must be supported and protected by the team leader.

You would turn white or purple, depending on your blood pressure, to see Helen wheeling one of your large file cabinets or taking a stack of your database disks out the door on her way to a new job with your competitor. Unless you have "backed up" her extensive knowledge in some way before she resigns, you are risking just such a lobotomy of core company knowledge.

HELPING TEAM MEMBERS RESPECT AND SEE BEYOND THE BOX

A team member in a corporate marketing department reported this situation: "Last month one of our team members brought along a self-described 'creative facilitator' to guide us (he said) in 'thinking outside the box.' After a long day pretending we were survivors on a desert island, architects of Tinker Toy bridges, first visitors to Mars, etc., we went back to work the next day pretty much unchanged and certainly unenlightened. Did we miss something?"

A large, well-heeled sector of leadership development consultants now line up behind the banner "Think Outside the Box." The phrase has gained the same kind of knee-jerk currency as the phrases "create competitive advantage" and "leverage human assets" from the 1990s. In their urgency to save us all from "the box," many consultants fail to understand how we got in the box in the first place and why we often prefer to stay there. When such consultants say "the box," they look as if they are sucking a lemon.

YOUR TURN

How would you describe "the box" of a position you now hold or a role you now play on a team or in an organization? How do you feel about that box?

_____

_____

_____

_____

_____

Does the Box Have an Upside?

But let's give the box its due. None of us are so far from our puppy days that we've forgotten the security of the box. When a new employee enters your business, he or she tries to grasp and practice all the rules, guidelines, and procedures that define a reliable, efficient company. Knowing the ropes of the firm is in fact nothing more than knowing the boundaries to respect—in effect, knowing the size and shape of the box of one's profession. There is obvious personal and professional comfort in such knowledge. We call it "knowing our job" or "having our act together."

INSIGHT 71

Although often disparaged, the imposed boundaries of one's job description or organizational role serve many useful and necessary purposes.

From the employee's point of view, the box can take the form of a written job description spelling out company expectations. Just as often, the box is a set of shared but unwritten expectations within a work group—who will do what to get the job done. The box can be a subset of technical knowledge within a specific business or industry. Or, the box can be categories on an annual or semiannual performance evaluation form. Any aspect of work life that tells us what we should and shouldn't be doing helps to create and enforce the walls of the box. We "know where we stand" thanks to the structure provided by our individual and corporate boxes.

From a leader's point of view, work gets done well when people respect their assigned boxes by staying on plan and within expected performance boundaries. Work often falls apart when people jump out of boxes by attempting to do others' jobs, ignoring policies, and inventing their own procedures. As a Pittsburgh network administrator put it, "My job is getting people in the company to do what they are supposed to—nothing less, nothing more."

In short, the boxes of job definition and adherence to company rules form the necessary foundation for order and efficiency within companies. Far from being the enemy of company success, the various boxes that describe procedures and policies make up the architecture of the company itself—a linked series of boxes, each performing its function on time and on budget.

YOUR TURN

Describe a time in your work or school life when it proved helpful to have a carefully defined "box" of performance expectations within which to achieve your goals and those of the organization. If your box in this situation had not been so carefully defined, what may have gone wrong in your efforts to perform? On the other hand, what happy surprises could have occurred in this less defined work or school environment?

_____

_____

_____

_____

_____

_____

_____

INSIGHT 72

Leaders may often be blind to their own boundaries or "boxes." Consulation with trusted peers, friends, and colleagues can help to reveal those limitations so that, if possible, they can be handled constructively.

The Limitations of the Box

Before we conclude this hallelujah chorus for the boxes of professional life, we should understand why a host of consultants urge us to escape such confinement. Here's a summary of their advice.

- *It's difficult to see over the walls of our individual boxes.* For all the advantages of knowing our assigned work responsibilities, we run into trouble when we are not able to see the big picture within the company. Certainly more than half of a manager's day-to-day job is getting people to see beyond their own schedules and priorities to the larger welfare, mission, and goals of the company.

- *The walls of our boxes may be closing in on us.* After an initial period of getting to know our assigned jobs, most of us want to feel that we are growing and developing toward new areas of interest and responsibility. Doing our 40-year stint at the same repetitive job isn't an appealing prospect. We don't want to "go postal" out of boredom and lack of initiative.

- *Boxes have an annoying habit of collapsing under stress.* In the fast-changing markets and economies of modern business, the work structures that made perfect sense yesterday may be a recipe for disaster tomorrow. Witness the yesteryear business models of K-Mart, Sears, Montgomery Ward (now defunct), Penney's, and other retailers who increasingly find their huge stores to be financial albatrosses. Many high-tech companies have faced the same kind of dramatic adjustment and reallocation of resources in adjusting a technology-based business to the roller-coaster expectations of the marketplace. When old boxes collapse, employees at all levels have to be able to adapt quickly to new ways of accomplishing work.

- *The worst boxes have lids.* Employees need to be able to look up, metaphorically, to imagine new career opportunities, untried solutions to company and customer problems, and innovative options for serving their own interests and those of the company. Exit interviews of bright workers leaving well-paying jobs are often replete with such explanations as "I just couldn't breathe in that job" or "There was no light at the end of the tunnel." Jobs without a future and without frequent problem-solving challenges can be dark boxes indeed.

YOUR TURN

Call to mind "the box" of a present or past position you have held in an organization. Describe ways in which you could have given more to the mission of the organization if the boundaries of that box had been expanded or removed.

_____

_____

_____

_____

_____

Thinking outside the box begins by thinking *about* the box, including its positive and negative influences on business life and individual career development. Playing desert island survivor games with a consultant is probably less valuable in this regard than taking half that amount of time to examine your own box, to measure its size by the yardstick of your talent, and to peek over the walls to see what lies ahead for you and your company.

INSIGHT 73

Leaders typically resist the restrictions imposed by "boxes" in their professional life. They should assume that talented team members are similarly impatient with arbitrary limitations, boundaries, and ceilings.

MEET A LEADER

Nathan Q.
Meals-on-Wheels Coordinator for House-Bound Seniors and the Disabled

"I am retired from my corporate job as an economic analyst. Frankly, I find my current nonprofit work much more interesting and fulfilling than my old job. The United States has no overall plan for feeding and caring for its elderly and disabled. Therefore, organizations like mine have risen up to try to do the right thing. In our case, that means providing a couple hot meals each day, a few minutes of conversation, and a reporting system to let other services know if we spot problems that individual clients are experiencing."

"As an economic analyst, I led a work group of 16 workers. I had to assign work tasks; check on progress; evaluate performance; and push, push, push to meet deadlines within our budget. That was one form of leadership, and I don't regret the experience. But in my present role, I notice a crucial difference: the people I supervise or coordinate really want to do as much as they can to help their clients. I don't have to motivate them by rewards such as raises and bonuses; in fact, just hearing about a particular client's problem can be in itself an incredibly motivating force for my people. I reported to one of my meal drivers last week that Mrs. Yont was experiencing bouts of depression. He took special note to stay a bit longer with her when delivering food and, as best he could, to help her focus on positive aspects of her daily life. I didn't tell him what to do. He initiated his own action plan because he cared about doing his best for his clients. I'm starting to understand that, with this kind of motivated crew of volunteers, my main function as their leader is to provide accurate information and to help share the specifics of each person's activities with the rest of the group. In a very real sense, they are the leaders and I'm more of a 'background guy' keeping things running smoothly. That's a very different experience from my days as a corporate leader, but I like the new experience."

Summing Up

Leaders can help team members become better participants at meetings, more insightful thinkers, champions and stewards of valuable knowledge, and key players who operate both inside and outside the boxes of their job descriptions. As the participation skills of team members blossom, the job of a leader becomes simultaneously more interesting and less burdensome. The single most important step to becoming a better leader is to involve oneself in developing better team members.

RECOMMENDED RESOURCES

BOOKS

Bennis, Warren G. On Becoming a Leader (Perseus, 1994).

Blanchard, Kenneth H., et al. The Little Book of Coaching: Motivating People to Be Winners (Harper, 2001).

DePree, Max, et al. Leadership Is an Art (DTP, 1990).

Flaherty, Jane S., et al. The Competent Leader (HRD, 1999).

Friedman, Stewart. Total Leadership (Harvard Business School Press, 2008).

Goleman, Daniel, et al. Primal Leadership: Learning to Lead with Emotional Intelligence (Harvard Business School Press, 2004).

Hamel, Gary. Leading the Revolution (Harvard Business School Press, 2000).

Kotter, John. Leading Change (Harvard Business School Press, 1996).

Kouzes, James M, et al. The Leadership Challenges (Jossey-Bass, 1996).

Maxwell, John. The 21 Irrefutable Laws of Leadership (Thomas Nelson, 1998).

Maxwell, John. Leadership Gold: Lessons I've Learned from a Lifetime of Leading (Thomas Nelson, 2008).

Northouse, Peter. Leadership: Theory and Practice (Sage Publications, 2006).

Rendall, David. The Four Factors of Effective Leadership (Rendall Associates, 2006).

Schein, Edgar. Organizational Culture and Leadership (Jossey-Bass, 1997).

Ulrich, David, et al. Results-Based Leadership (Harvard Business School Press, 1999).

INTERNET SITES ON LEADERSHIP

The Art and Science of Leadership: www. nwlink .com/~Donclark/leader/leader.html

Center for Creative Leadership: www.ccl.org/

Center for Leadership and Change Management: leadership.wharton.upenn.edu/

Center for Public Leadership: www.hks.harvard .edu/leadership/

Covey Leadership Center: www.ncrel.org/sdrs/ areas/le0cont.htm

Leadership Training Development: www .leadershipnow.com/

Leadership University: www.leaderu.com/

The Practice of Leadership: www.thepracticeof leadership.net

ENDNOTES

1. Warren Bennis and Burt Nanus, *Leaders, The Strategies for Taking Charge* (New York: Harper & Row, 1985), p. 116.

2. Quoted in James Kouzes and Barry Posner, *The Leadership Challenge* (San Francisco: Jossey-Bass, 1987), p. 81.

3. Piers Paul Read, *Alive* (Avon, reissue, 1992).

4. Quoted in Frances Hesselbein, et al., *The Leader of the Future* (San Francisco: Jossey-Bass, 1996), p. 74.

5. Noel Ticy and Ram Charan, "Speed, Simplicity, Self-Confidence: An Interview with Jack Welch," *Harvard Business Review* (Sept.–Oct. 1989), p. 54.

6. Michael Dell, cited in Dayle Smith, *The E-Business Book* (New York: Bloomberg, 2001), p. 94.

7. Douglas MacGregor, *The Human Side of Enterprise* (New York: McGraw-Hill, 1960).

8. John Schemerhorn, *Managing Organizational Behavior* (New York: John Wiley, 1998), p. 101.

9. Cited in Dayle Smith, *Eleven Keys to Leadership* (NTC/Contemporary, 1999), p. 57.

10. I. L. Janis, *Victims of Group Think* (New York: Houghton-Mifflin, 1972), p. 142.

11. Quoted in Dayle Smith, *Eleven Keys to Leadership* (NTC/Contemporary, 1999), p. 49.

INDEX